BAD FEELINGS

By the same author:

The Clinical Application of Psychological Tests

Psychoanalytic Interpretation in Rorschach Testing

Projective Testing and Psychoanalysis

Aspects of Internalization

A New Language for Psychoanalysis

Language and Insight: The Sigmund Freud Memorial Lectures
1975–1976

The Analytic Attitude

Narrative Actions in Psychoanalysis: Narratives of Space and
Narratives of Time

Retelling a Life: Narration and Dialogue in Psychoanalysis

Tradition and Change in Psychoanalysis

The Contemporary Kleinians of London (Editor)

BAD FEELINGS
SELECTED PSYCHOANALYTIC ESSAYS

ROY SCHAFER

OTHER

Other Press
New York

Production Editor: Robert D. Hack
This book was set in 10.5 pt Bookman by Alpha Graphics of Pittsfield, NH.

10 9 8 7 6 5 4 3 2 1

Library of Congress Cataloging-in-Publication Data

Schafer, Roy.
  Bad feelings : selected psychoanalytic essays / Roy Schafer.
    p. cm.
  Includes bibliographical references and index.
  ISBN 1-59051-046-1
  1. Psychoanalysis—Popular works. 2. Analysands—Conduct of
life. I. Title
  RC508 .S386 2003
  616.89'17—dc21   2002029254

To Rita

CONTENTS

ACKNOWLEDGMENTS

My greatest debt I owe to my wife, Dr. Rita V. Frankiel, and my good friend, Dr. William I. Grossman, from both of whom I have received the invaluable gifts of encouragement, sustained interest, helpful criticism, eager expectation, and appreciative response. I am also indebted to the many discussants and reviewers of earlier drafts of much of the material included in these pages; their responses to my journal submissions and presentations at psychoanalytic meetings gave me much to rethink and good reason to revise my preliminary efforts. I have used many of their suggestions. While preparing this book, I benefited from the editorial contributions of Erica Johanson and Bob Hack. Many thanks to Victoria Wright and Barbara B. Frank for their help in preparing the various drafts that went into the making of this book, and special thanks to Lanileigh Ting who prepared me technically and braced me emotionally for beginning to develop manuscripts on a word processor; without her cheerful help, this book would still be far short of completion.

I am grateful to the following copyright holders for permission to reprint here, as Chapters 2, 5, 6, and 7 of this book, material that first appeared in their journals: the *International Journal of Psychoanalysis* for "Disappointment and Disappointedness"; the *Psychoanalytic Quarterly* for "Defenses against Goodness"; and the American Psychological Association for "The Psychotherapist's Absence" and "Experiencing Termination: Authentic and False Depressive Positions," both of which first appeared in *Psychoanalytic Psychology*. Although I have introduced minor changes of content and organization in the interest of enhanced clarity, consistency of style, continuity of content, and reduction of repetition, the arguments of these papers has not been changed in any significant way.

INTRODUCTION

Troubled persons entering psychoanalysis depend on their analysts to maintain their analytic position through thick and thin. For unconsciously, and to some extent consciously, analysands are beset by painful feelings, one of which is hopelessness about being able to get rid of their emotional pain. Neither on their own nor with the help of significant others have they been able to change. Although analysands often seem to throw obstacles in the way of analysis, they do hope that their analysts will stand fast.

On their part, although they do have general guidelines that help them be consistent, analysts also try to learn in each case what constitutes leaving the analytic position, abandoning the analytic attitude, or, as it is said, breaking the frame. It may be offering reassurance, advice, or personal disclosures; it may be engaging in extensive questioning instead of listening to the drift of associations; it may be some or all of these and more. In the analysand's psychic reality, these deviations are likely to be experienced in one way or another as threatening. An attentive analyst can pick up the resulting signs of bad feeling even when, overtly, the analysands seem to fall in line and welcome the breaking of the frame: signs of loss of confidence in the analyst's security, strength, or clarity of vision; mistrust; and feelings of rejection, abandonment, anger, and despair. The analysand may never have formulated that need for an analyst who remains reliably in place. However, the analyst must be careful never to underestimate the urgency of that need.

"Bad feeling" can refer to every kind of painful feeling. It need not have any of the moral—more exactly, moralistic—connotations that "bad" takes on in other contexts: for example, "bad manners" or "bad character." However, unconsciously or even consciously, "bad feelings" *can* imply moralistic condemnation, For example, "It is bad of you to feel that way!" or "You're being a nuisance to worry about that!" There are those who, having been scrupulously brought up in families that have elevated mental health to the status of the Eleventh Commandment, believe that they are being bad when they have or express negative feelings. When they begin to feel anxious, glum, or ashamed, they are stricken with guilt or fears of punishment. In these instances, the analyst is witness to severe superego pressure for perfect adjustment. We might say, then, that mental health has become the cleanliness that is next to godliness.

Moralized mental health is only one source of the bad feeling of *guilt* or *anticipated punishment*, and these are only two of the many bad feelings that analysts encounter in their daily work. In this book I will highlight a number of bad feelings that are particularly painful. Because anxiety, guilt, and shame are so pervasive, both in human experience and in the clinical material to be covered in these pages, I will not devote entire chapters to them. I will emphasize humiliation and mortification (the extremes of shame); disappointment and, with it, disappointedness as a stance toward life; envy; abandonment; rejection; mournful loss; and the sense of dangerous vulnerability associated with experiencing one's own goodness or that of others and of making genuine progress toward maturity when that step has been anxiously or guiltily avoided for years. Despite its brevity, this list of bad feelings is long enough and the feelings it includes are sufficiently common and complex that, taken together, the chapters of this book have implications for the psychoanalysis of bad feelings in general.

One highlight of maturation is, of course, the development of defenses against painful—here "bad"—feelings. Consequently, the analyst's efforts consistently encounter not the bad feelings themselves but the defenses against them. Some of these defenses may be structured within pathological organizations designed to block feelings totally. In that case, the analysand may be understood as acting on the firm belief that sooner or later any feeling, even good feeling—happiness, confidence, enthusiasm, arousal, and so on—will bring on suffering. Chapter 1, "A Joyless Life," presents a clinical illustration of this extreme stand against feelings. Necessarily, then, this book has as much to do with defenses against feelings as with feelings themselves. Most likely the clinical analyst will be required to deal with compromise formations in which each constituent of the analysand's conflicts seems to have found limited expression, and that each of these constituents—including what appears to be simply defense—is loaded with pleasurable as well as painful feelings.

For the analysand to achieve genuine, stable, and adaptive emotional freedom, the analyst must maintain an empathic, respectful attitude toward the need for defense. Defense is not the enemy. It is essential analytic material as well as a necessary aspect of adaptive living. But because it may impede understanding of whatever it is that must be warded off, its strength or rigidity must be reduced, if extreme, before the analytic process can achieve comprehensiveness and stable, beneficial results. Thus, it is a major part of the analyst's job to attempt to work through that need for defense as much as possible—"as much as possible" because analysis cannot change everything. Under these conditions, the analyst had best beware the temptation to feel omnipotent and then humiliated or otherwise guilty for not being helpful enough. Manifestations of that countertransference inevitably add to the analysand's difficulties.

The reader will find what seems to be another set of compromise formations in both my mode of conceptualizing and my clinical approach to analysands. My discussions reflect my multiple grounding in Freud's writings, mid-twentieth century psychoanalytic ego psychology, and contemporary Freudian analysis, all of them modified by my keen interest in, and appreciation of the *clinical* approach of the contemporary Kleinians of London. I believe that, despite somewhat different terminology and technique, the contemporary Freudian and Kleinian schools of thought are closely related, like branches of the same tree—Freud—that are growing in somewhat different directions. I do not believe that my drawing on these varied sources is a kind of opportunistic eclecticism. As I will try to demonstrate, I view myself as responding to a deep harmony that has not yet been fully theorized.

This book is primarily clinical. I have tried to keep my remarks as down-to-earth as possible. My aim has been to help the reader find useful method and rich meaning in the analysis of bad feelings. To top things off, I have not neglected *the analyst's bad feelings* while at work. For example, in the final chapter, "Painful Progress," I develop a critique of one common and usually unquestioned concept that I believe expresses bad feelings on the analyst's part. Specifically, I challenge Freud's use of "negative therapeutic reaction" to characterize analysands' tendencies to back away from their analytic gains. Feeling bad can influence not only the analyst's interventions but his or her conceptualizations as well. I believe that the conceptualization of "negative therapeutic reaction" expresses negative countertransference. "Negative" casts a dark shadow over the analysis of inevitable shifts in the transference, a shadow that indicates that the analyst's preference or expectation matters more at that moment than understanding the analytic phenomenon at hand. Before that concluding chapter, I, too, will have used that well-established concept in various places, for instance, in Chapter 4 on envy. I do believe, however, that it is best to view the reactions in question in another way. When in a neutral position, the analyst does best to consider these phenomena to be signs that analysands are trying to regulate the kinds and rates of change that they are undertaking. Sometimes analysands believe it necessary to back away from what they unconsciously experience as too risky for them at that moment. Too much of their psychic equilibrium is at stake. When they do back away, they show the analyst that something more remains to be analyzed or that more time is required before an insight can be consolidated or a change in mental organization can be implemented and stabilized. I ask, what is negative about that?

CHAPTER 1

A JOYLESS LIFE

One of Freud's great contributions to psychoanalytic theory and technique was his constantly calling attention to the gain of pleasure concealed within the chronic psychical suffering that analysands present for treatment. It is now one of the chief aims of psychoanalytic work to interpret this gain in pleasure. To mention only a few examples of these unconscious pleasures: some analysands unconsciously maintain gratifying attachments to figures in their lives who, superficially, are presented as incontrovertibly "bad objects"; some, suffering from low self-esteem and complaining that they feel alone and helpless in a barren, persecutory world, get to be understood as satisfying their envious intentions to spoil actual or potential "good objects"; still others contrive to be punished as a way of assuaging their unconscious guilt feelings, in that way both enjoying relief from guilt and confirming their reassuring and pleasurable unconscious fantasies of omnipotent control.

It is well known that it is usually difficult to discern, bring to the analysand's conscious awareness, and work through these pleasure gains. Much of the difficulty stems

from the defenses that have been integrated into pathological organizations designed in part to protect these
secret pleasures. Additionally, the defenses themselves
can be interpreted as also providing unconscious sources
of gratification. For example, as a defense against feelings of loss, identification with the lost object relieves
painful grief while, in unconscious fantasy, it denies the
loss by keeping that object with one—as oneself; also, defensive regression from oedipal-level entanglements to anal-
sadistic modes of relationship simultaneously provides
unconscious opportunities to gratify sadomasochistic inclinations and allows one to continue oedipal engagements
in other terms, as when a son's tormenting obstinacy can
be interpreted as his carrying on a sexualized relationship
with his mother.

Freud's contribution is immeasurably helpful in analyzing those analysands (there are many of them) who
present themselves for analysis with the complaint that
they have been leading joyless lives. Though not hopeful
about change for the better, they do express the wish to
improve the quality of their lives. Often, they present a life
history characterized by a painful and emotionally deprived childhood; inhibitions of initiative, creativity, and
self-advancement; low self-esteem; and difficulty in forming and maintaining emotionally intimate and sexually
gratifying relations with others. Apart from low mood and
occasional irritability, these analysands usually show little
affect.

In this chapter, I will present some fragments of the
analysis of one such joyless man. The analysand, Ted, is
mentioned in several places in this book, each time in
another context and therefore each time differently thema-
tized. For example, disappointment, humiliation, and defenses against goodness, each of which figured in Ted's

analysis, are emphasized in one place but not another. Taken together, these interrelated examples can be regarded as illustrating the major technical concept of *working through*. And as in working through, some repetition of life historical and descriptive material is unavoidable.

TED

Ted came to analysis complaining that his life was drab, his mood low, and his capacity for social and sexual relationships markedly limited. No longer a young man, he was unhappy about being unmarried and childless. His self-presentation was notably devoid of affect. Ted's parents, now deceased, had fled political persecution in a Mediterranean country after members of their family had been imprisoned or killed. Subsequently, they appear to have lived frightened, secluded, depressed lives.

Over the course of Ted's analysis, it became possible to interpret unconscious pleasures he gained through his ostensibly empty emotional life. For example, it was possible to interpret to good effect a strong involvement in sadomasochistic manipulation of others. He showed this involvement especially clearly in his relationships with women. Repeatedly, he disappointed them. He accomplished these disappointments by setting up battles with them over commitment that he could be sure of winning. More than winning, Ted was also proving to himself that he needed nothing from them. His sense of security and unconscious omnipotence depended on his projecting his own needfulness into these women and then viewing them as grasping, predatory, and devouring. To insure his victory, he was quick to find fault with each woman, especially if he found her interesting or physically attractive.

3

Thus, Ted had become a master of contemptuous invulnerability and implied self-satisfaction. Remaining oblivious to the pain he caused by his aggressive, demeaning, even torturing strategies, he never showed a flicker of guilt. In his conscious self-concept, he was blameless. It was just that, as he saw it, there was nothing and nobody out there for him.

After several years of analysis, Ted was able to acknowledge that he played a game with others: he saw "how close to the edge" he could maneuver them before making propitiatory gestures that drew them back to him and led them to expose themselves to further disappointment at his hands. Sometimes, in telling about this game, Ted would smile with satisfaction; occasionally he even felt gleeful, as when he told how he could just walk away from any involvement with another person.

Much of this understanding developed from the analysis of the transference. Because it was on his own that he had come to analysis for help—and he did come faithfully—I could assume that genuinely, though secretly, Ted hoped to give up at least some of this manifestly lonely, unhappy, and unconsciously cruel controlling life. In the consulting room, however, repetition was the order of the day. For years I was treated as just another demanding invader to be warded off, another would-be seducer he could thwart and possibly lure into disappointment. For example, he could lead me to feel hopeful about change for the better (in his terms) only to then shut his steel doors abruptly in my face. He did this by forgetting, minimizing, or becoming even more toneless after any brief period of engagement during which he showed that he felt impressed by me or drawn to our work or to me. For him, feeling those ways implied that I might be a good person who would then have the power to disappoint him. All the more reason then to repel me. In his defensive mode, Ted needed me so that he could play the game of disappointing me and rejecting me in his almost incredibly bland and oblivious manner.

At the same time, Ted was careful to pacify me. He did not want me to give up on him altogether. From early on, as though reassuring me, he would report how much the analysis was benefiting him. He would give examples drawn from his extra-analytic life of increased involvement, inner reactivity, and overt expressiveness. These "progress reports" did not seem fabricated; however, because for a long time they led to no change in his transference or in the kind of "dead" material he typically kept mulling over during his sessions, they seemed to be still too much in the service of dulling me and seducing me into disappointment.

Later in Ted's analysis, I realized that the way he behaved—his emotionless, omnipotent sadomasochism—was far from the whole story. For example, it was his way of demonstrating fanatical loyalty to idealized versions of his parents. Indeed, he was behaving as though they were still alive, still overly attached to him, and still vulnerable to any emotional shifts away from them; unconsciously, he imagined that if he were to form a sustained, gratifying emotional relationship with someone else, it would kill them. It was not only that he was identified with their lifelessness; in their roles as introjects, they were living, clinging figures, always present in the consulting room, just as they always came along on his dates. Although Ted was not delusional in any usual sense of that word, his loyalty to these imagoes seemed to be one of those private, nonmalignant, encapsulated delusions that are developed by so many of those who have suffered severe early narcissistic damage and whose functioning has remained split between the concreteness of unconscious fantasy and a well-developed capacity for abstract, rational thought.

5

Their good sense of reality remains intact so long as they avoid intimate relations with others.

Ted lived out this role by adopting the lifestyle of a near recluse, mostly keeping to his own home, remaining isolated at school and later at work. He could not ask for recognition and so was usually just taken for granted. Although he performed on a high level with what appeared to be commendable organization, he could do so only under the condition that he was meeting a specific assignment, never when he was required to pick a topic of his own and develop it in his own way. Doing things in his own way implied selfishness, what others would call leading an independent, affirmative life in which he would be looking out for his own interests, too. He was required to live quietly and unnoticed *with* and *as* his dead parents.

Taking Ted's fanatical loyalty into account, I began to view him as desperately seeking to avoid consciously experiencing profound guilt feelings. That he was successful in this regard was evident in his apparently guilt-free manipulation and persecution of others. The potentially painful layer of guilt was, I thought, connected with the possibility, mentioned earlier, of killing his parents by forming good relationships with others. Even showing clear desire was forbidden. He had learned early in life that, along with bearing disappointment without complaint, he was to see no evil, hear no evil, and speak no evil. He was to "make no waves" by wanting things, by feeling enthusiastic or frustrated, or by asserting self-interest as a normal child might. Except for critical reactions, anything felt spontaneously was excessive and unworthy.

Also, guilt was associated with his fantasy that he had already killed his parents. He had killed them long ago by adopting a withdrawn position at home. He had minimized his dealings with his parents and allowed himself little

conscious feeling for them. Thus, his transference was enacted in his shutting out any sign of feeling about me. In
this way, Ted was repeating his deadly attack on them at
the same time as he was being true to them.

This combining of seemingly opposite aims also served
as a defensive way of saying simultaneously, "I'm sorry
and I'm punishing myself" and "I don't care!" "I don't care!"
was one of his frequently repeated responses in words,
shrugs of the shoulder, or smirking responses to the efforts
made by others, including me, to help him confront the
damage he was doing to himself and to them. In one and the
same gesture he could be sadistic and pay the price for it.

Ted's case had now taken on the tragic cast that analyses do once they have made substantial progress. Its tragic
nature was obscured by his self-concept as a blameless
person and his social presentation as a soulless person.
Especially noteworthy in this respect was Ted's general
unresponsiveness to the drama of language. He drained
his language of color. He leveled it to the point of flatness.
Generally, he was unresponsive to my variations of emphasis through my spontaneous use of metaphor, simile,
or mild exclamations. Later in analysis, after Ted had begun
relaxing his controls and defenses a bit, he was able to complain about my not having colluded with his purging language of all feeling. He claimed that my use of language had
been "too exciting, too demanding of emotional response."

Ted could not convey this complaint all at once. First
there was only a dream of someone breaking through a
wall in a distressing way. After I deciphered the transference complaint in the dream, Ted could agree in his flat
way that he had resented my expressive language, which, I
should mention, rarely dramatizes issues that come up
during analytic sessions. Yet, by letting me know that my
limited spontaneous expressiveness was too much for him,

7

he was conveying that when he is exposed to excitement and surprise, he feels on the verge of "a riot of emotion." In this context, he dreamed that he was endangered by an imminent avalanche. Consequently, he had to live "in a cocoon" in the analysis, as elsewhere; the alternative, he felt, was "catastrophe."

Ted also had many ways of maintaining his strong barriers against depending on others. Not only was dependency a humiliating contradiction of the omnipotence implied in his ascetic self-sufficiency, it overexposed him to emotional stimulation. He showed this defense in the transference by the way he handled my bills. He always paid them the day after he received them. He handed me his check without looking at me. When he could, he just dropped his check on my desk as he passed it on the way to the couch. In this way he avoided the "touch" aspect of money passing between us.

I understood this behavior to be expressing anal-sadistic and anal-erotic tendencies. Among other things, he was apparently influenced by intense but secondary anxiety about homosexual tendencies that paralleled his mistrust of women. Primarily, however, I inferred that Ted was determined to prevent his developing any indebtedness to me. He was to leave no trace of his having received services on which he counted. He was to give no hint of desire to hold onto his money or to hold onto me by delaying payment. He was to show no pleasure in paying me lest it be taken as felt gratitude, adequate restitution for his array of attacks on me, or expressions of intimacy that might also imply sexual feelings. In short, I was not to become a good, exciting person in his life.

As is regularly the case in analytic work, much of this material could be interpreted only after Ted had begun to change. He did change, typically with much backing away from any new development. This defensive backing away expressed more than anxiety; it showed him to be continuing his efforts to disappoint me so that I, too, would experience the despair that he seemed to have been feeling ever since childhood. Nevertheless, the more conscious he became of his set of strategies and the beliefs and feelings on which it was based, the more he began to feel faint traces of incipient affection, enthusiasm, remorse, and constructive commitment. These feelings appeared last of all and least of all in the transference because, up to the end, he could not participate actively or openly in direct work on his "unrelated" relationship with me. Mostly he explored fragments of transference in cooled-down, intellectual terms.

As I mentioned, the changes for the better that did take place were more evident and openly gratifying to him in his extra-analytic life. Despite these limitations, I began to believe that Ted was genuinely acknowledging my importance to him and his belief in the truth of my transference interpretations. Although there seemed to be signs everywhere of the power of his omnipotence, his sadomasochism, his need to reject dependency and avoid guilt, they had diminished in number and magnitude to a noteworthy degree. He no longer had to lead me on to the extent that he had earlier.

With these changes, Ted was allowing pleasure to enter his personal and occupational life. He could successfully and independently analyze his own assaults on his newfound moments of happiness. His sense of reality having been cleared of many of his projective identifications and other primitive defenses, he could perceive and remember the good side of others and his need for them; he could be good to them on numerous occasions, and he could imagine a pleasurable future without immediately or lastingly filling it in with fear of impending disasters or finding—more exactly, creating—flaws that spoiled any chance of gratification. This was as much as he could offer himself and me, and for him it was a lot.

DISCUSSION

One might ask whether or to what extent it was borrowed guilt (Freud 1923) that was exerting a major influence on Ted's retreat from overt, socialized forms of pleasure. Although it could be assumed to begin with that he, like the rest of us, could not emerge from childhood free from residual guilt feelings, it did seem that Ted was carrying an unusually heavy burden of guilt and was striving mightily to keep it out of consciousness. There were many reasons for this outcome, but it is reasonable to suppose that one of them was his parents' suffering greatly from their own survivors' guilt and their having atoned by living subdued, "dead" lives. If so, Ted would have grown up believing, among other things, that love and loyalty to his parents required him to lead their kind of life. He would have done so out of compliance, identification, defense against retaliatory rage, and a wish to protect his miserable parents. It seemed, however, that the pain of this guilt was too heavy a burden for him to bear consciously, so that he constructed a pathological organization of desire, defense, reparation, and need for punishment that could effectively cancel out conscious guilt feelings. Unconsciously, he could then view his pleasure-giving sadomasochistic manipulation of others, his isolation, and his manifestly joyless life as being "in a good cause." Change from this position could be contemplated only with dread.

The life-historical account of Ted's life and present position that we co-constructed through interpretation further suggested that Ted's parents not only needed him to stick with them; they also expected him to seek their advice and help and to receive these parental gestures gratefully. He played his part dutifully but unemotionally. It was all a matter of going through the motions of aliveness and relatedness, and he did the same in his transference.

Access to this strategy was gained through his becoming able to acknowledge that, mostly secretly, and just as he had occasionally derived pleasure by tormenting his mother over petty details, he was trying to get at me. For example, there were many times when he made it difficult to be understood even superficially, and other times when he steadily negated or modified my comments. Also, he would often introduce complications in his schedule of appointments. In part, he was intending to be at least a nuisance, if not severely frustrating and enraging. Expectably, these devices enabled him to stir up negative countertransference, the self-analysis of which helped me understand better the carefully disguised oedipal aspects of the tormenting games he played with his mother.

That borrowed guilt played a significant part in Ted's pathological organization seems to be an interpretation with some merit. If so, it could be helpful in understanding other anhedonic lifestyles. And, as will become evident in the chapters that follow, disappointment, humiliation, and defenses against goodness can play equally important parts in constructing joyless lives.

CHAPTER 2

DISAPPOINTMENT AND DISAPPOINTEDNESS

Disappointment is an inevitable, pervasive, more or less painful, and perhaps traumatic experience in almost every phase of life. As a central feature of the Oedipus complex, its influence is powerful, far-reaching, and lasting. Hidden pockets of profound disappointment insidiously limit significant aspects of development, sometimes blocking them severely.

Beyond influential individual experiences of disappointment, analytic interest must extend to *disappointedness* as a fixed, hardened attitude toward life in general. That attitude expresses itself in a grim view of what life has offered and a bleak expectation of what the future holds. It includes the determination that life must not be allowed to be anything but disappointing. Then, disappointedness has become a goal in life—one might say a career. Upon analysis, hardened and insistent disappointedness is often understood to serve aims that are simultaneously defensive, aggressive, and, as in moral masochism particularly, libidinal. Also to be taken into account is the overlay of defenses that may have been erected against exposing oneself both to feeling one's disappointedness and, what is worse, showing it.

Certainly, references to disappointment pervade clinical case reports; however, when analysts have addressed disappointment itself, they have taken up this important topic under other headings. These headings include depression, mistrust, frustration, and masochism. Consequently, disappointment does not appear in titles of papers, and it is not indexed in the work of Freud and others. Three exceptions to this trend should be noted. First, Jacobson (1946) contributed an early and excellent paper on disappointment. Although she mentioned disappointment frequently in her subsequent work (1964, 1971), she tended to subsume it under *depression.* Bergler (1948) took up disappointedness in his well-known work on "injustice collectors," a group he described as eagerly seeking disappointment; however, he situated this emphasis within his general study of superego pathology. Finally, Joseph (e.g., 1989, pp. 117–120, 127–128, 174–178) usually discusses disappointment under the more general heading *despair.* The present chapter is offered as a supplement to these three contributions. It focuses on detailed manifestations of the experiences and activities in question, including rigid defenses against them.

I will discuss disappointment under several conventional analytic headings: disappointment as a reactive feeling, as a defense, as a weapon, and as a sought-after form of suffering that may yield secret pleasure. I will also consider disappointment in relation to adaptation, in this regard emphasizing its useful potential under extreme circumstances. Later on, I will present a clinical example that illustrates some of the ways in which these aspects of disappointment entered into the treatment relationship between one analysand and one analyst. Because I have not undertaken to present a complete case analysis, only some of the sexual and aggressive trends in the analytic work will enter into the discussion.

FEELING DISAPPOINTED

Ordinarily, people feel disappointed when experience fails to be in line with strong wishes or confident expectations. This response is so regular and considered so natural that it usually does not come up for direct and intensive scrutiny in analytic sessions or reports. Of greater analytic interest are all those instances in which accounts of having had some wish gratified or having reached some goal are followed by, "It didn't live up to my expectations," "It wasn't as good as I thought it would be," or "I had hoped for more." Reflective writers of essays and fiction have urged us to realize that the excitement might lie more in the chase than in the capture or that the joy in the creative process lies more in working creatively than in the work's end result. André Gide wrote somewhere that the first touch of a hand could be more exciting than the later full-fledged sexual encounter. Some have even counseled that if we do not get our hopes up, we will never be disappointed. Here, the analyst must ask, "What is this all about?"

IDEALIZATION

To a significant extent, it seems to be about idealization as a built-in component of every strong desire. Although idealization can serve a useful function by arousing and sustaining interest and by increasing one's tolerance for delay of gratification, in the end it will impose a price on those same advantages. That is, it will have led us unrealistically to expect some bliss that is fully uninhibited, unambivalent, and untouched by elements of displeasure. We discover then that we have been dreaming the dream of pure fulfillment, transcending ourselves, and soaring into that realm of pure pleasure that we seem destined never to enter except perhaps in the first flush of fulfillment or expectation. Only later might we realize the extent to which our idealizations have entailed denial of complexity and also how omnipotent fantasies have played significant supporting roles in our initial, seemingly unalloyed thrills. Infatuations have these complex features (Freud 1921).

In our analytic work, we might construe these idealizations as springing from infantile layers of our being that continue to foster fantasies of total, uncompromised fulfillment. Ordinarily, Freud's (1915c) omnipotent "pleasure ego" has been more or less mastered in the course of development; the reality principle and secondary process have usually come to hold sway over this ineradicable infantile state. Freud's (1905, 1937) recognition of these features of development never deterred him from emphasizing the imperishability of the infantile unconscious. However well prepared we may be for the miseries of everyday life (Freud 1893–1895), we continue to be subject to the enduring influence of these primitive imperatives. On this basis, idealizations, denials, and omnipotent fantasies will have been constructed and sustained with the help of many projective identifications: specifically, projections of one's own narcissistic fantasies of the magical self and corresponding grandiose images of the "good objects" and "bad objects" of one's infancy (Freud 1914a, 1915c).

The disappointment that so often throws its shadow across pleasurable experience seems to rest on still more factors than those already mentioned. Looked at in terms of life history, this shadowing might spread from negative aspects of childhood. These aspects would include painful memories of frequent disappointment, loss, the forbiddenness of certain forms of pleasure-seeking, or the avoidance of pleasure owing to conflictual, threatening circumstances that involve expectations of painful consequences, such as fear of the envy or collapse of a depressed parent.

Looked at in terms of the present, the shadow might also spread from the looming threat of feeling destructively greedy or envious of the goodness of others to the point of wanting to rob them or spoil the very objects on whom one depends (see Chapters 4 and 6). Difficulties are increased by competitiveness, an ambivalent stance toward stirred-up dependency feelings, and excessive projection of bad parts of the self into potentially good objects. One example would be the defensive analysand who cannot accept the analyst's goodness wholeheartedly, if at all; projects "bad" feelings into the analyst; and then experiences the analyst's empathy as contempt, contemptible weakness, or seduction.

In reaction to these developments, the analysand may regress to some crudely narcissistic, perhaps manic enclave of fantasized omnipotence from within which he or she can safely deny totally the worth and the joy of any good experience. One might deny these pleasures because acknowledging them would conflict with well-established guilt-ridden feelings of undeservingness, with other high-priority defenses, or with old, treasured, and nursed grievances toward the person who now seems to have become a good object.

The developmental gain through psychoanalysis in this context of disappointment is acquiring and valuing a perspective on the inevitability of imperfection in that which one holds dear. Analyses that have gone well help develop a potential for making allowance for imperfection in pleasure without radically diminishing one's capacity for love, hopefulness, enthusiasm, and dedicated effort. That potential to make allowances rests on decreased reliance on splitting and projective identification, more reliable reality testing, greater differentiation and stability of object relations, an increased steadiness of goal-directed activity, and a tolerance of high spirits. At the same time, that potential for tolerance contributes to the further development of these ego strengths themselves. Thus, this process of development feeds on its successes.

It seems that making allowances is an essential ingredient in the capacity to endure the ambivalence that Klein (1940) highlighted as a marker of entry into the depressive position. In Kleinian analysis, this tolerance is recognized to be one of the achievements of leaving the paranoid-schizoid position (Klein 1946) sufficiently to be able to begin to work through and maintain some approximation of the depressive position. Working toward that position does not mean the end of conflict but rather a flexible and resilient integration of one's own mix of psychological maturity and immaturity.

DISAPPOINTEDNESS

Those analysands who develop fixed, hardened attitudes of disappointment have usually suffered prolonged, severe deprivation and pain in their early object relationships. The deprivation and pain might have been inflicted by violence and extreme poverty; however, they might be attributable to continuous neglect or abuse of emotional needs stemming from parental inhibition, depression, psychosis, physical illness, or harsh child-rearing practices that presumably favored total self-reliance and self-control but produced the opposite results. Alternatively this disappointedness might have been constantly reinforced by a steady diet of humiliation ostensibly designed to make sure that one never brings shame on the family. As will be discussed in Chapter 3 on extremes of shame, the key phrase in this context tends to be "knowing one's place." Analysis often strongly suggests that this diet of humiliation is aimed to reduce the chances that one will threaten the brittle defenses and shabby self-esteem of others in the family whose envy has been aroused by one's significant achievement and self-confidence.

Analytic studies of reactions to violence, deprivation, and humiliation are not, however, controlled by simplistic and totalistic theories of inevitable and uniform reactions to these traumatic impingements. Analysts investigate as closely as possible how each child internalizes these experiences and transforms their meanings and status in accord with each successive stage of development. Experience in the world counts for a great deal, of course, but so does the fantastic nature of the child's immature and often uncomprehending psychic reality, a worldview that regularly persists into adult years. It is an essential part of the analytic task to try to establish how the affected child has both accommodated to and come to use these painful experiences for libidinal, sadomasochistic, defensive, and moralistic purposes. Of equal interest is how, over time, each child has made corresponding alterations in the ego functions of reality testing, anticipation, and frustration tolerance. For analysts must presuppose that these changes continuously shape and reshape fantasies about oneself, others, and the possibilities of human relations. Also, the changes intensify or diminish the influence of these fantasies and enlarge or narrow their scope.

Being thus prepared to give due weight to layered unconscious mental processes that mediate "real experience in the world," analysts make few suppositions about the obviousness and severity of those events that have helped produce disappointedness. Instead, they recognize that children in such contexts as parental favoritism, serious illness, unavoidable separations, physical injuries, or parental loss will construct unconscious fantasies appropriate to their total situation, and these fantasies may then play powerful roles in each individual's psychic history. Consequently, analysts further assume that in most cases it is difficult if not impossible to establish in great historical detail "what really happened" and "what really mattered." They must work with life history not decisively but in a provisional manner. For analytic purposes, what matters is the analysand's hardened attitude and fixed and embittered modes of constructing experience. Influential access to these crucial factors is gained principally through interpretation of the transference and the countertransference.

References to libidinal and aggressive aspects of disappointedness and to modified ego functions will pervade the following discussion; their defensive and moralistic aspects have been singled out for special mention. In each respect, I will present extreme instances that highlight the important variables; however, one should not forget Freud's repeated reminder that in practice one is always dealing with considerable flux, compromises, and residual ambiguities.

DEFENSIVE DISAPPOINTEDNESS

In its defensive aspect, chronic disappointedness is directed against hopeful expectations of a world inhabited by good objects. These objects are now dangerous because they expose one to new disappointments and ensuing fruitless rage along with a painful sense of betrayal or of having been cheated. The defensiveness is often expressed consciously as a profound fear of and aversion to dependency. In these instances, *dependency* is being used to derogate attachment to others of any sort. The goodness of others—their generosity, forbearance, forgiveness, and love—is mistrusted, minimized, dismissed, or reinterpreted as a narcissistic form of gaining control and gratification. One fears that recognizing even the possibility of gratification will intensify rage at disappointing internal objects, usually the parents. All the more is this the case when, in unconscious fantasy, it is believed that these objects must be viewed as benign in order to protect them.

Consequently, analysts get to understand that they are encountering fixed constructions of a world without true goodness, though it may contain a certain amount of "protective" attributions of goodness. To further this defense, the disappointment-prone analysand intensifies attachments to bad objects, thereby validating her or his bleak strategy. Moreover, that analysand might also be consistently provocative in ways that are certain to bring out "the worst" in others. Analysts' analysis of their own countertransferences repeatedly lends support to the interpretation that they are being subjected to more or less veiled assaults on their analytic goodness.

MORALISTIC DISAPPOINTEDNESS

Hardened disappointment also has its moralistic potential. It can be used to point an accusing finger at the presumably good objects now viewed as unreliable. These objects are then made to seem betrayers of hope and seducers of the unwary. They create expectations that are certain to cause frustration. In this stimulation of guilt, or at least doubt, in others, there is much projective identification. Studies of masochism have emphasized its uses for this kind of moral censure of these "bad" others.

The second moralistic aspect of hardened disappointment is its expression in attacks on oneself, resulting in abject feelings of undeservingness and harsh criticism for being too demanding, too greedy, too dependent, too vain, too unappreciative. One becomes disappointed in oneself in response both to having been failed by others and to having projectively reduced them to bad objects on the strength of one's own fear and hatred. We see this in the analysand who is sure that he has come to his appointment at the wrong time, when in fact it is the analyst who is keeping him waiting; false protectiveness is likely to be part of this reaction. The analysand who feels undeserving of the analyst's attentiveness, appreciation, and understanding may be using this same strategy.

Unconsciously, both moralistic forms of defense tend to include a pleasurable aspect: the pleasure (mixed with relief) in suffering itself, supplemented by a triumphant sense of victory—victory achieved triply by implicitly playing three parts: a harsh judge of others, a benign protector, and a profound disappointment to them. In *Masochism in Modern Man* (1941), Reik wrote of masochism as a way of achieving victory through defeat.

ADAPTIVE ASPECTS

There can be an adaptive aspect to fixed disappointedness. For example, when a child is forced to endure a harsh, punitive, frustrating life, it could be adaptive for him or her to conclude that, under the circumstances, hoping for anything better will lead only to repeated bouts of rageful depression and painful demoralization. That child might conclude that it is better to adopt disappointedness as a protective wall of resignation or despair.

This strategy for survival leads to the maladaptive consequence that it can long outlive the awful circumstances in which it seems to have originated. Many analysands come to realize during their treatment that, in their adult years, this strategy has become primarily, if not exclusively, a self-fulfilling prophecy. The despairing orientation did help them survive the emotionally horrible years of childhood spent in extremely dysfunctional families; beyond that, it could even have sheltered the flickering flame of a candle of hopefulness from the harsh winds blowing about it. Analysands learn that they have shielded themselves against reality testing and put constraints on object relations in order to maintain this despairing stance; further, they have buttressed this defense with a pathetic idealization of the past and with other tendencies already mentioned, such as self-incrimination, self-denial, and self-defeating relations with others.

TRANSFERENCE

The analysands described here enter analysis deeply committed to disappointedness in the analysis itself. Typically, they approach the analysis and the analyst well armored against a transference of any kind—more exactly, of any other kind—for this armoredness is, in fact, their initial transference. Later on, one way in which to defend against any other transference feelings is by idealizing past times in their analyses—for instance, the initial interviews—

when their now-disappointing analysts had been "warmer," "kinder," "more involved," or "smarter about things." In a different defensive mode, they might idealize their analysts in the present as "different" from others, and therefore no proof of a better world outside the analytic relationship. However, this limited expression of appreciation often proves to be brittle, for sooner or later, after seemingly slight provocation, these analysands will turn on their analysts as cheats and betrayers of hope, acting then as if unmasking a long-suspected enemy.

Freud's continuing emphasis on the fragility of the neurotic positive transference has been amply borne out over the years. Here, I am adding that a readiness for, or a need for, disappointment is a likely contributor to this fragility. Also, as mentioned, these analysands are likely to try to induce a variety of disruptive countertransferences, thus bringing out "the worst" in their analysts and validating their own grim expectations. Because projective identification seems to play such a large role in this effort, it is warranted for us to pause here to consider in some detail its role.

PROJECTIVE IDENTIFICATION

Projective identification is used during analysis to validate fixed attitudes. Bad internal objects and bad aspects of the self are attributed to the analyst's self. So much may this be so that the analyst will be tempted to conclude, "I'm damned if I do and damned if I don't." The analyst might even be rendered unable to get out of this bind, at least for a while, but sometimes permanently. In another tactic, projective identification may be used to get rid of feelings of disappointment, in which case the analyst will be experienced as disappointed in the analysand if not also in his or her life as an analyst or life in general—a reading of the situation that might touch on some of the analyst's sensitive personal issues. In a further move, the analysand might buttress this projective position by self-denigration and ideas of being an unrewarding patient, thereby "justifying" the analyst's presumed negative attitude.

On their part, analysts do at times tend to project one or another manifestation of their own countertransferential disappointment into their analysands. They might then manipulate them into corresponding enactments. It will all be much the same as in certain parent–child relationships in which the children have been saturated with the projections of their parents' own disappointments—disappointments with themselves, their own internal parents, their spouses, or their careers. The analysand will have become the "designated disappointee" in the family, and, subsequently, the "designated disappointee" in the analysis. Analysts often discover through countertransference analysis that these victims of parental projective identification have gone on to better their instruction.

When Freud (1923) referred to borrowed guilt, he mentioned only the child's unconscious identification with the father's guiltiness. I would venture to suggest, however, that a seriously guilty parent of either sex is likely to have already projected much guilt into the child, thereby contributing significantly to the appearance of the child's "borrowing" (see also Chapter 8 on the so-called negative therapeutic reaction). That is to say, the genuinely borrowed elements can sometimes be seen as stemming from the parent's projective identifications having played into the spontaneous guilt feelings generated by the child's immature fantasies of desire and destructiveness. Viewed in this light, this guilt is not so much borrowed as it is a joint achievement within the family. By becoming the "disappointing" one in the analytic transference, the analysand repeats the same pattern that Freud described in connection with superego analysis.

IDEALIZED MEMORIES

Idealized memories were mentioned earlier in this chapter in a passage on transference defense. Idealized memories have often been taken up in cultural studies, for example, with reference to past times as "golden ages." In the present context, the analysand might set up fantasies of powerful nostalgia to contrast with painful feelings of disappointment in his or her current life. In this way, idealizing the past might also serve an adaptive function, that is, it might help to sustain hopefulness and determined efforts to make things better "again." Apart from providing relief from current painful experience, one's turning to comedies, love stories, and romantic adventures might also serve auxiliary functions of keeping alive hopes for the future.

More often, however, analysis suggests that these idealized memories and fantasies are being used defensively to justify intense disappointment in the present. The strategy is that of contrasting what is present and expected with a glorious edenic past: a past free of ambivalence, pain, and uncertainty; a past in which people felt secure and authentic within themselves and in their families and community; a past when everything was simpler and better.

CLINICAL EXAMPLE

In this example, we return to Ted, the analysand discussed in Chapter 1 as leading a joyless life. Much of Ted's analysis lends itself to being retold in terms of disappointment: disappointment *in* others and himself, his being disappointing *to* others, and particularly his guarding against feeling desire or taking initiative lest he expose himself to the pain of disappointed expectations. This thematic material was implied in a pathological organization or psychic retreat (Steiner 1993) comprising defenses, secret gratifications, aggression, self-punishment, and partial adaptations to many painful circumstances in his present life that seemed, through analysis of transference, to be of his own making. This pathological organization seemed to be layered, each layer defending against the dangerous layer below it. For instance, the repression of desire and initiative served to ward off his consciously experiencing his disappointedness. So far as it worked, this defensive layer allowed him to be relatively emotionless. He lacked spontaneity and was ready at the first sign of conflict or dissatisfaction to retreat from budding attachments or even the possibility of forming attachments.

As already described, Ted lived a relatively withdrawn life. In his work, he was conscientious and competent. His surface layer of virtual apathy was buttressed by, on the one hand, heavy reliance on projective identification of feelings and desires into others and, on the other, idealization of his extraordinarily disappointing parents. He found it painful and guilt provoking to say anything at all about his parents. Even to describe them was regarded as criticizing them. The least hint of criticism was "disloyal." Thus, the analyst's expressions of interest in Ted's developmental history were most unwelcome, and for a long time any interventions designed simply to clarify the distinction between his objectifying his parents and his attacking them proved to be futile. For him, it was a step toward recognizing how disappointing they had been and his reactive rage and depression.

27

It was later, after much of the story had been developed, that the many ways in which Ted's parents had introduced painful disappointments into his life could be formulated. It became clear that his attachment to both parents had many of the features of attachment to bad objects. It also became clear that his settled attitude of disappointedness had served the adaptive function of sparing him further pain. Additionally, he had turned passive into active with the help of projective and introjective identification, in that way becoming himself a steady source of disappointment to "possessive" others, a strategy that also yielded him aggressive, sadistically tinged satisfactions.

Also mentioned earlier was Ted's being especially disappointing to women, first getting their hopes up about his developing a serious interest in them and then becoming passive, withdrawn, and too ready to feel dissatisfied. On occasion, he would fleetingly experience some sadistic pleasure in leaving others dangling from their hopes as he failed to come through for them. In this respect they were being treated vengefully, most of all as disappointing mothers.

These tactics entered into the transference Ted constructed. In some respects, I could quickly recognize this transference and handle it appropriately. Sometimes, however, I could recognize it only through the countertransferences that he could stimulate. For example, confronted by this maze of idealization, projective identifications, affectlessness, and subtle reversal of passivity to activity, I would sometimes find it difficult indeed to maintain patience when seeking to work out interventions that would gain access to Ted's psychic retreat.

But beneath these two layers there seemed to lie a third layer of hopefulness. This layer could be inferred from Ted's having come to analysis on his own, seeking relief from feelings of depression and loneliness as well as expressing a fading hope that he might just develop a lasting, pleasurable relationship with a woman and enjoy having a family of his own. Although it soon became apparent that inwardly he had mobilized his resources to thwart me, he came regularly to his appointments, and although he used any sign of change for the better to try to get my hopes up prior to disappointing me by sudden reversals, he also seemed briefly able to genuinely value these usually small advances. It became clear as well that Ted had to spoil these pleasures-in-progress by soon surrounding himself with doubts about their genuineness and by engaging in little enactments that corrupted them. In this way he created a steady stream of disappointments in himself. Fundamentally, it seemed, he was reassuring himself that he was not making himself vulnerable to large-scale disappointment. Some of these doubts about the genuineness of change had some basis; others appeared to be pure spoilers in the service of self-protection.

Throughout, his defensive maneuvers conveyed both a desperate need for gratification of dependent needs and a terrible fear of just that eventuality. It was this fear that contributed to his projecting into others, especially women, an aggressive, greedy possessiveness and a need to control and dominate. It also led him to develop unconscious omnipotent fantasies according to which he could be totally self-sufficient. He sustained these fantasies by leading a life in which his needs were few. His lifestyle severely limited the possibilities for disappointment.

Years later much had changed. Although his vulnerability to disappointment had not disappeared, he could tolerate and partially, hesitantly, enjoy serious and lasting relationships. He was able to lead a significantly more socialized life. Also, by this time he was suffering much less apathy and depression, and there was less of that need for omnipotent control that fundamentally denies the separateness and the autonomy of all the others that one secretly cares about or depends on.

Thus, Ted had made significant progress out of the depths of a paranoid-schizoid position and moved tentatively, erratically, and only so far into the depressive position (Klein 1940, 1946, Steiner 1993). That this advance had retained an unstable, tentative, and partial quality was evident in the difficulty he continued to have in fully experiencing his relationship with me or thinking freely about it. At the time of the session I will now present, Ted was beginning to change at a pace somewhat faster than the glacial pace that had characterized the first years of analysis. The session centers on paternal transference.

Monday: Ted comes in feeling unusually upbeat. He is eager to tell about how different this weekend had been from the way weekends were "several years ago." (Note that in keeping with his show of not needing others, he says, "several years ago" instead of "since I've been seeing you.") Ted gives details. He had been to church. He had gone on an "okay" date with a woman. He had attended a big picnic arranged by his firm and then gone to dinner with some of the picnickers. On Sunday, he had also gone to a ball game with some of them, even though, he adds, he is not a sports fan. To top it off, he had even met an interesting and responsive woman with whom he might try to go out the following week. In the past, he emphasizes, he has never been able to get so interested, be so gregarious, or take that much initiative.

Then Ted tells three dreams of Sunday night.

Dream 1: *A carpenter working on the analysand's apartment had removed some flooring and replaced it with floor-*

ing that was more modern in style. He was very angry with the carpenter for not maintaining the traditional tone of the apartment. He felt betrayed and angry enough to think of not paying the man. He added that the carpenter in the dream had in fact once worked in his apartment.

Dream 2: *He was holding a man's hand. He thought that there must be something homosexual about this dream; however, when asked about it, he could not say whether he had had that thought in the dream or only afterwards.*

Dream 3: *He was getting on a bus and there was much pushing by the crowd of riders, so that some got on without paying. He was debating whether to do that, too, or to pay. In the end, he got on without paying. The man of dream 2 seemed to be on the bus, too.*

For a while, Ted ruminates about that repairman in dream 1. He says that the actual job had worked out quite well. His hopes had not been dashed.

Analyst: It sounds as though now you are mad about something or feeling betrayed in some way.

Ted (thinks about this): Nothing comes to mind.

Analyst: I think the only man who is working for you right now is me. I've been doing a kind of reconstruction job with you. It could well be that in some way you feel betrayed by me and mad at me. Perhaps you have mixed feelings about the personal changes you've been reporting. From all the work we've done this far, you would know that you are ambivalent in this regard. In the dream, unlike in your opening of this session, you could be showing that you are also angry about changing away from your old, better-protected ways.

31

Ted: I can see that, but it seems too simple; the interpretation needs more depth. [In this there was a direct assertiveness that contrasted with his tendency of old to ignore my comments, disagree with them, or, most of all, mull them over while qualifying them and amending them in so many ways as to seem to take them away to an isolated place and leave me feeling alone and perhaps having failed to give him a good interpretation.]

Ted then associates to the ambivalence he had felt toward his father in connection with having frequently confided in him; he had resented this show of dependence on his father. (Mention of this ambivalence is not new. It had been taken up in the past more than once.) Then he mentions his impression that his father's availability for confidences was based on the father's own needs, too; specifically, he needed to maintain the appearance of being a good father when confronted by obvious gaps in his attentiveness. Ted resented his father's being in it for *his own reasons*. (This point was mainly new.)

Analyst: It must be that way with your feeling dependent on me for these changes that are taking place. You would be mad at those things that make you feel more hopeful, even mad enough not to want to pay me. I think you resent the idea that I'm in it for reasons of my own, such as getting paid for it. Holding a man's hand in the second dream could refer to your relationship with me and its unwelcome implication of dependence.

Ted (accepting this idea, though now only in a flat, ungiving tone): Now the interpretation seems adequate. I didn't want to pay in the first dream either. Now I'm getting tearful.

Analyst: I think it's painful for you to contemplate that you would have angry feelings toward me when you are also grateful to me for the positive changes you've been telling me about. It could feel like biting the hand that feeds you.

Ted: I can see your point, but the tearfulness came without my feeling anything of a deep sort at the moment, so that I am still somewhat puzzled by it.

Next, Ted thinks of an incident from the time when he was a young adolescent. He had told his father his fears of sexual inadequacy, and with a few words his father had reassured him about it. On his part, he had not been too happy about having had to go to his father in the first place. It was not so much that he was humiliated as that he shouldn't have needed the reassurance at all. He added spontaneously that it was the same in the analysis.

Ted: There is a layering of negative feeling here in the analysis that bothers me: the first layer being that I am dependent, the second being that I would admit it, and the third being that I would end up resenting it. Now I am sort of outdoing you in interpreting the dream [said self-consciously and with anxiety]. I can see here that the prototype of my relationship with you does seem to lie with my father.

Analyst: So it seems. It's time to stop for today.

DISCUSSION

Because I was thinking mainly about Ted's having split his ambivalence about changing, I did not realize at the time

33

that, by Ted's changing as he was, he would feel he was betraying me by going too far. That betrayal would consist in his making progress away from a dependent position and even "outdoing" me. In the dream, he would have been defending against the resulting guilt by projecting his treacherous feeling onto me in the role of the modernist carpenter who "goes too far." Upon reflection after the session, I thought it would have been better to convey to him his own culpability—as in his "outdoing" me—and how he tried to rid himself of it. I had missed his guilt of persecutory anxiety.

At this point in the analysis, neither Ted nor I feared that the dialogue in this session would cancel out, or throw into question, the extent to which his transference included maternal as well as paternal elements. Both of us had been moving back and forth, considering both transferences, sometimes together, sometimes independently, for these did have distinct as well as overlapping features. The two of us were beyond being preoccupied with being too specific. Partly, this eased attentiveness was a consequence of his father's having had to take over many conventionally maternal functions during Ted's development, his mother apparently having been a rather withdrawn, unreliable person during his early years.

From one point of view, Ted's struggle both toward and against overt, mature independence and competence was an outstanding feature of this session. Because objectifying his parents represented a step in that direction, he felt guilty about "going too far." Objectifying them still retained some sense of giving up his idealization of them and separating himself from them in his internal world. To him, becoming autonomous still aroused anxiety of guilt over his abandoning them and harming them. He was not yet free of feeling it was disloyal, a betrayal, destructive. In this respect it was not me but Ted himself who was the betraying "modernist" carpenter; his criticism of the carpenter was also projected self-criticism.

As for his idea of the dependent father, it did not seem to be pure fantasy based only on projective identification. To a significant extent, it seemed clear that on some striking occasions, his father actually had clung to him emotionally. Moreover, his father had felt frightened and hurt on those scattered occasions when, in his adult years, Ted acted as though his life was primarily his own to live as he wished. Ted was beginning to confront the fact that his father's self-serving clinging lay in the background of his own fear that I was primarily looking after myself. What he had been showing in this session was how his own dissatisfaction, anger, and assertiveness had only heightened his guilt. By acting in his new way, he was being a wretched ingrate as well as a disloyal and abandoning son both to his father and his analyst; hence, his fears.

Looking at this session from the point of view of disappointedness, one could say that the complex dynamic arrangement that had protected Ted from disappointment in his father and me was beginning to yield to interpretation. Ted was showing the extreme bind he felt himself to be in: acknowledging both dependent and independent feelings and exposing himself to painful disappointment, hopelessness, grief, guilt, and rage. Much of Ted's disappointedness, especially in his father and in his transference, warranted and unwarranted, was at this moment still too painful to acknowledge freely.

It complicated matters further that his increased awareness of his separateness confronted him with two disagreeable prospects: having to tolerate envious and angry feelings (biting the "good" hand that fed him) and recognizing that the sense of omnipotence he maintained in his withdrawn world was coming to an end along with some reduction of his attachment to bad objects. Now, there would be distinct and potentially disappointing others in the world and he would need them, and his self-isolating shows of independence (unconsciously, his omnipotence) would no longer constitute a workable solution. Ted was on the road to a mature form of autonomy, but it was still so steep and rocky, and it still entailed so much pain, that he could not move ahead without much distress and defensiveness.

CHAPTER 3

FORMS OF EXTREME SHAME:
HUMILIATION AND MORTIFICATION

Psychoanalyzing experiences of extreme shame brings to the fore unconscious fantasies dominated by degrading, violent, and deadly themes and imperatives. It is inevitable that these fantasies play important roles in deciding the forms and emotional tones of our human relations. I have singled out for special attention two manifestations of extreme shame: humiliation and mortification, both of them outstanding manifestations of bad feelings.

The degrading and violent fantasies that give humiliation and mortification their special qualities include ostracism and death, excrement and rejection, the annihilating consequences of losing face, desperate recourse to compensatory omnipotence, and internalization of bad objects that have actually been encountered, created out of whole cloth by projection, or projectively exaggerated during early development. These fantasies can be inferred and interpreted on the basis of the transferences that analysands construct to cope with their extreme shame in the analytic situation.

Although mention will be made of contemporary Freudian and self psychological approaches to shame, no detailed reviews, comparisons, or critiques will be attempted here. In some places, however, my discussion will overlap or show the influence of these other approaches.

OSTRACISM AND DEATH

Humiliation and mortification frequently involve unconscious fantasies of disgrace and ostracism. One feels excluded from one's community after having totally lost its respect. Being ostracized often implies dying emotionally or spiritually as a result of one's having been made to feel a nonperson, worthless, or an unwanted substance. The implied loss of spirit and corporeal death is implicitly recognized and expressed in everyday figurative language: "I could've died from shame," "I could've sunk into the ground," "I've been dumped on," and "That was the end of me."

These death-tinged fantasies are etymologically rooted. The word *humiliation*, derived from humus or earth, shifts in common usage through "on the ground," and "of the earth," to "lowly" or "low-down." Thus earth, which can be associated with birth, growth, and fertility becomes an illustrative instance of what Freud (1910) called the antithetical meaning of primal words; for now, earthiness implies death, removal, and decay.

The same theme is restated in the case of the word *mortification*: think of the words mortal, immortal, and mortuary and the phrase mortal combat, and again you enter the fantasized realm of death, dying, even killing. Mortification is usually represented as an internally generated experience, one based on harsh self-judgment; in contrast, humiliation refers to being shamed painfully by others. However, the distinction between the two experiences can be blurred in such instances as mortification experienced as the result of an attack by an internal object rather than by the self. Another kind of blurring results from one's projecting the mortified feeling and then feeling humiliated.

EXCREMENT AND REJECTION

Feeling humiliated by others is often expressed in some variation of this complaint: "I was treated like shit." Shit is often prominent in the unconscious fantasies associated with humiliation and mortification. Freud (1905) and Abraham (1921) showed that these painful experiences often express anal fantasies. Traditionally, the linkage of extreme shame to anality has been thought to develop especially around the time of early habit training, particularly toilet training. Optimally, that training is designed to carry only the message that one is being trained to be appropriate, well socialized, clean, regular, and healthy. The intended emphasis is on adaptation: the importance of being an acceptable, respectable member of the community, most of all with that special community, the family. However, in unconscious fantasy, excrement can be a weapon, an explosion, and a murderously powerful regulator of self-esteem, a source of sensual pleasure, a gift and a form of sex (Freud 1909). Consequently, the message received and transformed by the child being trained can vary greatly with age and circumstance. In any case, we encounter here another instance of the antithetical sense of primal words. Consider, for example, the destructively dismissive expression, "I don't give a shit," which disavows all concern for, even interest in, the other or oneself. Here, excrement is represented as doing both good and bad in the world.

Calling others assholes is another example of our equating humiliation with excrement, and the case is the same when we say they acted in a crappy way or what they are saying is bullshit. By bringing in ideas of waste, filth, stink, and refuse, we render our target lifeless and deserving only to be rejected in disgust. To be "shit on" signifies provocation to feel despair or to enter into a sadomasochistic transaction. "Garbage" and "junk" are euphemistic forms of anal derogation. Like the others, they imply rejection, fit only to be thrown out or thrown away.

LOSING FACE

Feeling humiliated or mortified implies the painful experience of having lost face. Although many of the implications remain the same as those already mentioned, the manifest emphasis shifts from the anus to the face. The idea of face also has many cultural and developmental implications concerning prestige and honor, discussion of which will be bypassed here in favor of what usually gets to be featured in analytic, often body-oriented interpretations of losing face.

On primitive levels of thought, it is believed that, if one's face is not seen, one is not being seen at all. Thus, *losing face* can be a devastating experience in that it implies that one has lost identity by having been abandoned, utterly devalued, or finished off. In contrast, *saving face* implies continuing to exist or, in hard times, at least salvaging what life is left in you and rejoining what community remains available to you.

Defacing is associated with losing face. Usually, defacing refers to marking up something to spoil it, make it ugly, and deprive it of its existence by making it so changed as to be unrecognizable, unacceptable, strange, alien, even harmful to look at—thus, like excrement, something worthless, repulsive, even dead. At the extreme, *effacing*, like erasing, denotes total destruction by elimination.

Viewed in this context, the common reaction to humiliation and mortification of hiding one's face is likely to express penitent disclaiming of worthiness, vitality, or presence—ultimately, the death and disappearance implied by "sinking into the ground." Unconsciously, hiding one's face can also signify covering or burying the disgusting excrement with which you now feel identified. In a sense, it is an act of *ef*facing, that is, giving up your subjectivity to get rid of the painful bad feeling. When "faceless," you may be unconsciously enacting your death and burial—annihilation. It may also be a gesture that signifies trying to ward off being defaced by another, thereby defending against a killing blow.

In general, then, the hands that cover the face unconsciously create a scene of violence, repudiation, death, and disappearance. However, at least in our culture, the implied catastrophe is also negated for you remain present and seen, and your hidden face can always reappear intact. Thus, the gesture can signify resurrection from the death enacted by the characteristic gestures of humiliation or mortification.

Viewed most broadly, these are instances of the unending psychic contest in unconscious fantasy of life against death. Like spring after winter in mythology, life is being affirmed by showing your face once again. You have been punished or have been penitent long enough. Nothing is final. Persecutors can be pacified. Traffic moves in both directions.

When their shame is extreme, analysands live with the fantasy of always being looked at disapprovingly. Sometimes they put it put in terms of being seen through by others, implying an experience of nakedness with nowhere to hide their badness. Then, shameful experiences of long ago may be remembered so vividly that it is as if they are happening here and now. Being profoundly self-conscious, these analysands are hyperalert to the environment's actual or projectively imagined or intensified disapproving responses. As mentioned, much of the disapproval and rejection is likely to be emanating from internalized bad objects and only then projected. Finally, these unfortunates are cut off from looking to themselves for affirmation and constructive criticism; basically, they cannot observe and judge themselves independently.

TRANSFERENCE

These analysands rapidly and rigidly experience their own excessive self-criticisms as emanating from their analysts. In doing so, they rely heavily on projective identification. They hope thereby to get relief from the pains of an internal world of extreme shame and persecution. By attributing their bottomless dread of humiliation or experienced mortification to the actions of others, they hope to be able to change their circumstances, for then they might be able to subdue these others or flee from them. During their analytic sessions, having emptied themselves of their own dire expectations and bad feelings, they may act as though they have no minds of their own. Their analysts will have to do all their thinking for them.

On their part, their analysts soon recognize that these analysands are acting out fantasies of persecution at the hands of overinvolved hypercritical, unappeasable, unreachable sadomasochists. For a long time, these analysands feel that they are under close, hostile, continuous surveillance, and they take all interventions as confirmation of their worst fears, that is, as having been found out, or as condescension, insincerity, accusation, or commandment. Alternatively, they might construe benevolent neutrality as evidence that their analysts' judgments are worthless. They will be safer that way—they hope.

Analysands who live with humiliation and mortification are situated within the paranoid-schizoid position (Klein 1946). Emotional experience and concrete thinking take precedence over symbolic thinking and focused concern for others. They show no readiness to feel guilt when appropriate. In both respects, they lack the characteristics of those who have moved toward or into the more integrated, whole-object-related, thoughtful depressive position (Klein 1940). From within this transference, the analyst is approached or avoided with paranoid dread. These analysands feel so transparently undeserving, rotten, or shitty that, unconsciously, they expect their analysts to react to them hatefully and treat them with disgust, ever ready to abandon them and consign them to spiritual as well as corporeal death and decay.

Drastic experiences in the transference of this sort are not captured by the words embarrassment, feeling foolish, chagrined, or gauche. Nor do inferiority, inadequacy, or simply being uninteresting do it. Only the words for extremes of shame, such as humiliation and mortification, will do. The damage done in unconscious fantasy must not be minimized.

ENVY

Envy can play an important role in stimulating or intensifying humiliation and mortification and its expression in transference (see also Chapter 4). The envious wish to spoil is often accomplished by humiliating looks, gestures, or words. Envy can destroy the other's own sense of personal worth, making her or him feel like excrement or refuse (Klein 1957). Those who feel spoiled by envy say such things as, "I was made to feel dirty," "It was terrible of me to make such a spectacle of myself," and the like. Along the same lines, envious friends or family members often try to spoil an analysand's enthusiasm for or tolerance of treatment and the changes it is bringing about in the way they live their lives, and when they are successful, the analysand often comes to subsequent sessions feeling that the analytic approach or the analyst is rotten or untrustworthy.

The basic difficulty, however, lies in the envy the analysands feel toward their analysts, envy that they often do their best to hide or project into others. They feel that their analysts possess what they lack themselves: goodness, integration, sanity, power, and happiness. Defensively, some of them may split off these idealizing assessments, ascribe them to themselves, project their envious selves into their analysts, and then imagine themselves to be coping with envious analysts. At this point, they might experience their analysts' interpretations as envious efforts to make them feel worse, to think even less of themselves than they already do. No longer picturing themselves as spoilers but rather as victims of their analysts' spoiling intentions, they go on to try to stimulate their analysts into countertransference responses of disgust and rejection. In this effort, they use even the slightest sign of real or imagined departure from neutrality and acceptance to validate and intensify their sense that they have innocently entered into a bad relationship and exposed themselves to a steady stream of bad feelings.

OMNIPOTENCE

When envy enters into situations of extreme shame, grandiose fantasies of the self are likely to be in play, too. Opposites meet: vulnerability and omnipotence. The grandiose fantasies must be protected from the analyst's transference interpretations. No sense of being flawed, deficient, or powerless must be allowed to develop. These analysands become intolerant of the virtues and assets of others. Enviously and spitefully, they try to spoil the goodness of others so that they themselves will not have to cope with their own sense of smallness, ugliness, weakness, and inferiority. Neither loss nor guilt must be allowed to enter their scenes of operation, and so too with needfulness, dependency, and powerlessness. In effect, feeling godlike, they imagine being able to give birth to themselves and nurture themselves in a totally self-sufficient manner.

All of this constitutes a defensive, devaluing attack on the analyst and his or her interventions. This grandiosity can be expressed quite subtly. For example, the analysand might too readily assume total responsibility for experiencing humiliation, thereby precluding complaints against others for having contributed to the problem or having stimulated the bad feeling; consequently, the opinions of others, analyst included, need not matter. Total mortification blocks out any sign of envy and resentment. This kind of self-blame does not signify or lead to a developed sense of responsibility, for it does not take into account the capabilities and feelings of others. The thinking is concrete and entirely self-referential; words, looks, and gestures are being treated like missiles and shields. In the end, however, nothing has changed except perhaps the painfulness of the moment; the distressing internal world has not been eliminated. In this grandiose setting, the unconscious fantasy might even include dying gloriously at the center of the (analytic) universe, perhaps meeting a saintly fate (on the couch). In any event, the narcissistic, paranoid-schizoid position continues to predominate.

CLINICAL EXAMPLES

Carol

Carol was profusely apologetic for having a critical thought about her analyst's clothes. She sounded as though she had inflicted so much harm that she could rightfully expect serious retaliation. Her contemptuous thought seemed to have stemmed from her unconscious identification with a mother she had experienced as scornful of everything and everyone. Most of all she had identified with a certain pained expression she believed she saw whenever her mother looked at her. Unconsciously, she was seeing the analyst through her mother's contemptuous eyes, to some extent at the behest of her mother as internal object and to some extent as identification with this object. To deal with her mortified state, she was projecting her fragile, vulnerable, humiliated, but also envious and vengeful child-self into the analyst to support her precarious conscious sense of strength, worth, and superiority. In this instance, she was disguising her envy and omnipotent fantasy by becoming apologetic. Pleading weakness diminished her fear of retaliation. Saying that you are sorry doesn't necessarily mean that you are feeling guilty.

Ed

Ed's expression of contempt for his unsupported idea of his analyst's reactionary politics was also tied to identification with a mother he had experienced as contemptuous. However, he could not integrate his feminine identification and had been trying desperately to exclude that "female" self from consciousness. Characteristically, he hid behind a superior "masculine" self-representation that included a good deal of arrogant, implicitly omnipotent behavior.

Sam

Sam was hiding from himself and others his noteworthy assets in the realms of intelligence, charm, sense of style, and perceptiveness. On the strength of projective identification and seemingly realistic perception, he believed his hiddenness would protect not his self-esteem directly but rather the self-esteem of his parents. In these respects, they appeared to him to be limited, fragile, and potentially envious. They also seemed intolerant of intimacy. Analysis of Sam's transference helped him withdraw some of his projections and gain access to a number of suppressed assets. He felt freer than ever before to develop them further. He became more adventurous and imaginative, and he felt livelier in his sexuality. Fear of humiliation and mortification played a smaller part in his life.

Sharon

Sharon was extremely vulnerable to feelings of humiliation and mortification. Much of the intensity of these feelings had developed in the consistently shaming environment in which she had grown up. Her self-esteem had been crushed by judgmental, persecutory responses to her spontaneity, self-assertiveness, and individuality. She identified with her aggressors and put herself down so consistently that, feeling mortified or, if she resorted to projective identification, feeling humiliated, seemed natural to her. Unconsciously, she tried to compensate by exaggerating normally present omnipotent fantasies and expressing them in exasperated, contemptuous, judgmental, persecutory attitudes toward others. She was always ready to blame them for their shortcomings and blunders. Also, Sharon could not tolerate being dependent on others, especially if they were different from her in their interests and values. In her transference, she alternated between unworthiness and superiority.

Expectedly, Sharon felt that being in analysis was humiliating. It made her "so ordinary." One day she appeared with a cast on her foot, having broken a small bone in a fall. She reported that she was aware of having felt a bit of a shock when she was shown the x-ray of her toe. She reflected that it was "so ordinary" to have a skeleton like everybody else and to be vulnerable like them. "It's degrading!" All her compensatory fantasies of being special were threatened by this confrontation with her humanness, her existential vulnerability.

DEVELOPMENTAL AND INTERPERSONAL INFLUENCES

Humiliation is often inflicted on others—as it was on Sharon—in the form of such challenging questions as, "Who do you think you are?" The question need not be put into words; it may be conveyed by such gestures as raised eyebrows or mocking looks. When parental figures repeatedly confront a son or daughter this way, they stimulate the child to internalize them as demeaning bad objects and perhaps to go on to identify with them and become a persecutory figure of that sort themselves; this in addition to their constantly, even if secretly, being self-deprecatory. Humiliation and mortification become a way of life.

Feeling thoroughly humiliated or mortified, these children unfailingly "know their place" and carry that burden on their backs into their adult years. That place is lowly, marginalized, perhaps seen but not heard, and certainly lonely, but behind the scenes they also sit on high, harshly judging others. One such analysand revealed that his case was so severe in this respect that he had approached his initial interview prepared to throw himself at the analyst's feet and beg for mercy. This dramatization betrayed his concealed arrogance.

The defensive advantage gained by identifying with the aggressor, real or imagined, is feeling relatively safe from unexpected criticism. Already victims of strain trauma, these analysands feel particularly pained by criticism for which they are unprepared. It is important to "beat others to the draw." This shoot-out metaphor and others like it suggest the unconscious fantasy of the deadly violence of having felt traumatically shamed.

Directing the question "Who do you think you are?" at oneself also works against stirring up the envy of others. You cannot be envied for what you successfully disavow. Yet another defensive advantage of seeming to remain small, humble, and humbled is in its helping to maintain vigilant defenses against gross manifestations of your reinforced latent grandiose tendencies. In developing his self psychology, Kohut (1977) strongly emphasized the not uncommon need of analysts as well as analysands to defend against idealization by others that threatens to overstimulate their latent grandiosity. Better then to dwell in shame or shrink into excessive modesty. Various metaphors of conceitedness imply this fear of grandiosity: swellheaded, too big for your britches, and too good for this world.

A price is paid for adopting this strategy of internalizing the humiliating attitude in addition to readily feeling humiliated. You become ever more envious of others for their freer and fuller achievements, the ease of their relatedness to others and their being "out front" about their assets, their self-assurance, and the multiple pleasure possibilities open to them. Additionally, unless you are exceedingly careful, you will somehow betray your judgmental attitude, begin to be regarded by others as nasty and haughty, and possibly suffer ostracism. Also, you will view your community as one crowded with failures, isolates, betrayers, deserters, and persecutors. With everyone and everything having been leveled to the ground—or lower—you end up feeling lonely and desperate, with a sense that life is meaninglessness.

Further disadvantages include the damage you do to your own development. By inhibiting use of your capacities, warping your reality testing of your actual achievements, and splitting yourself by always having to be on guard against the spontaneity that might reveal your own enviable talents, assertive self-interest, or pride, you stunt your development, your social relations, and your career. Then, there is little possibility of your being recognized by others as an enjoyable, worthwhile, or interesting person. You have few if any experiences of normal pride. You live as though you have assigned all self-definition and self-appraisal to others. You are totally vulnerable.

DISCUSSION

Humiliation and mortification are not simple affects. They are understandable in terms of splitting, primitive narcissism and aggression, projective identification, envy, and grandiosity—in short, the features of the paranoid-schizoid position. In some respects, my account of these two extreme experiences of extreme shame departs from what has become traditional in the ego-psychological Freudian literature on shame. That literature is exemplified by a set of papers in *The Psychoanalytic Study of the Child* (Ablon 1990, Abrams 1990, Gillman 1990, Yorke and collaborators 1990). These scholarly, clinically knowledgeable, informative, and useful essays adhere faithfully to Freud's now superseded metapsychology of instinctual drives; they approach shame, and implicitly its extremes, as though affects are irreducible components of instinctual drives, and as though these components acquire their ideational content as the child moves through the psychosexual stages of development. These are the stages during which the child constitutes an ego, ego ideal, and superego, and achieves self–other differentiation. Thus, for them, as for Freud and contrary to contemporary theories of emotion, cognitive elements are not intrinsic to affective experience.

Although content similar to that emphasized earlier appears in these papers, it does so in a somewhat different context. These authors, too, emphasize loss of control, dirtiness, inferiority, and a sense of physical or mental exposure, but exposure, for example, refers primarily to phallic-oedipal conflict over exhibitionism, voyeurism, and masturbation and not to the major dyadic issues of early development. This difference makes plain what is well known: the extent to which the traditional ego-psychological literature subordinates pregenital issues to phallic-oedipal interpretation, especially of a positive libidinal sort. This traditional emphasis continues to be

51

present in more recent publications than those already cited (for example, Rizzuto 1991, Rothstein 1994). It contrasts with the growing trend today toward an emphasis on early object relations. This trend does not exclude what has been traditionally explored; it's just that it goes deeper into primitive levels of experience and fantasy. Some of these recent developments stem from the heuristic potentials of the self-psychological approach. For the most part, however, my discussion has been stimulated by the work of the contemporary Kleinians (Schafer 1997a,b).

Whatever the approach, it is always important to remember the extent to which concrete thinking characterizes primitive unconscious fantasy and infuses the experiences of humiliation and mortification. Freud would have had it so despite his metapsychological abstractions and segregation of idea and affect (1915a); one has only to read his work on dreams (1900) and danger situations (1926) to see that this is so.

As noted earlier, this concrete thinking shows up in our figurative language. There, for example, although we speak of feeling "like dirt" or of our "dirtiness," formulations that derive from a conceptually and self-representationally higher level of thought, when using these terms we also implicitly identify ourselves with dirt, garbage, or shit. Being told, "You're a piece of shit," "a dumb cunt," or "a big baby" is, in unconscious fantasy, taken literally. We see indications that this is so in dreams, slips, and symptoms. Similarly, the experience of inferiority has its concrete representations in unconscious fantasy in terms of physical attributes and actions pertaining to victimization and brute power, size of sexual and other body parts, and so on. Ultimately, there are the variously imagined danger situations of annihilation and death.

One technical consequence of these considerations is this recommendation: it is helpful to be sparing in one's use of interventions beginning with "as if" or "like," because these formulations will likely require analysands to shift to a higher level of psychic organization than the one they are on at that moment, the result being failure to capture the most deep-seated painfulness of the bad feelings then under analysis. More effective analytically in many instances are simple declarative statements, such as, "I think you are feeling defensive now, believing that I'm critical of your attitude" or "My comment made you anxious, and you are trying to change the topic to a safe one," provided that the analyst is simply straightforward in speaking so and not overbearing. Being too hypothetical or indirect does not help, usually.

CONCLUSION

Humiliation and mortification come together as prominent members of a family of bad feelings included under extreme shame. Either term may extend as far as a sense of worthlessness and annihilation associated with fantasies of deserving to die, being made to die, even causing oneself to die. But in the manner of unconscious mental functioning, with its tolerance of magical and contradictory possibilities, these fantasies and the gestures and figurative language that correspond to them also imply retention of the power to reverse the process, thereby to regain existence and acceptance through penance and rehabilitation, and possibly even to fantasize exercising omnipotent control over others.

It cannot be emphasized too strongly that feelings of humiliation and mortification and the fantasies of which they are an indication are built-in aspects of being in analysis. They pervade defensive efforts and are conductive to negative therapeutic reactions. But there is an opposite side to that coin: the use of humiliated and mortified feelings as defenses against expressing envy in the transference. It is to envy that we turn next.

CHAPTER 4

ENVY: REVISITING MELANIE KLEIN'S "ENVY AND GRATITUDE"

Envy has come into its own. Contemporary psychoanalysts are actively discussing and debating the varieties of envious experience and their origins and influence (see, for example, Britton 1989, 2001, Frankiel 2000, 2001, O'Shaughnessy 1999, Spillius 1993). That it has not always been so is well known. For many years, envy had been locked up in a box called *penis envy*. The box now opened, envy is being conceptualized in a manner both more complex and more wide-ranging in implication. Among the factors responsible for this change, two stand out: the creative work of Melanie Klein (1957) in her classic "Envy and Gratitude" and the critical acuity of scores of feminists who have wanted to free psychoanalysis from its phallocentric bias. It is from Klein's classic that many of the ideas set forth here are drawn. To these I will add some thoughts and observations of my own, together with those to be found in many instructive feminist writings. With envy finally being seen by analysts to be the ubiquitous problem it is, the beneficial analytic consequences of this enriched insight cannot be overestimated.

I begin with a brief account of how I understand Freud to have arrived at the insight that penis envy plays a central part in the development of girls and the lives of women. For this development, whatever its flaws and undesirable consequences, has retained great value in theory and practice, and it remains the context into which significant change is being introduced. Because I have already critiqued Freud's general theory of girls and women at length in several places and in several ways (Schafer 1974, 1992, 1993, 1994, 1997c, 2001, among others) and because my aim here is to provide a contemporary approach to envy, I will not present a detailed review of these works. Instead, after completing this introductory section on penis envy, I will focus on the work of the contemporary Kleinian analysts who have been refining and adding to the analytic efficacy of so many of Klein's (1975) ideas on theory and technique. The place of envy in transference, countertransference, and family relationships will receive special attention.

FREUD AND PENIS ENVY

It is well known that Freud (1925) emphasized the fateful consequence of the little girl's discovery of the anatomical distinction between the sexes: immediate penis envy that persists and becomes a central reference point in both her psychical development and her mature life. As one of the major bad feelings of human beings, this envy plays a part equivalent to castration anxiety in men. It is implied that the mere fact of *difference* is a major stimulant of envy, an implication recently elaborated in Frankiel's (2000) discussion of the general role of difference in stimulating envy.

Over the years, Freud's interpretation of penis envy has proved to be too narrow. I believe that this narrowness resulted from the way he situated this anatomical difference in the grand scheme of human existence. Specifically, Freud pressed it into the service of his leading preoccupations: heterosexual development, reproduction, and the continuation of the species (Schafer 1974). In the background of this preoccupation were Darwin's great contributions to the origins and survival of species. That Freud was under other influences to be discussed later—the industrial revolution and the patriarchal social orientation of his time—contributed its share to the role he assigned to penis envy.

Because Freud (1940) stood pat on this interpretation, even after he tried to expand it (1933), it remained for other analysts to challenge his narrow vision. For example, Karen Horney (1924) contributed at an early date to expanding the study of envy by developing another model of female development. In her model, however, penis envy played a part that, even though secondary, remained much like Freud's. Also, in the light of later developments, her perspective, like Freud's, can be considered narrow owing to its predominant oedipal conception (Schafer 1974). The content of Horney's formidable challenge to Freud's apparently unquestionable authority was not widely accepted or emphasized by most analysts, the dominance of Freud's formulation virtually blocking further thought on this important topic for a long time. But Horney did open the way for reconsideration and revision.

Several subsidiary factors played a part in arresting further development in this major sector of psychoanalysis. One factor was analysts' tendency to subsume manifestations of envy under *rivalry* and *competition*, these being variables that fit into the oedipal configuration. Also, Freud's conception subsumed envious experience under a sense of personal defect or inferiority caused or exaggerated by neglect, assault, and punishment for sexual "badness" such as masturbatory activity. And third, Freud's having made the triangular oedipal situation the center of his theories of development and neurosis contributed to insufficient attention being paid to influences emanating from preceding stages of development. This was so despite Karl Abraham's (1924) work and despite the significance of these stages having long been recognized by Freud (1905).

MELANIE KLEIN'S CONTRIBUTION

Later developments, spurred particularly by the work of Melanie Klein (1957), focused on the *dyadic* relationship with the mother in the years before the height of the Oedipus complex. Additionally, Klein developed a fuller account than Freud had of the often dominant role of aggression throughout development, and she did so in a manner consistent not only with what Freud had written in "Instincts and Their Vicissitudes " (1915c) and "Beyond the Pleasure Principle" (1920), but also in the line of thinking developed by Abraham (1924) about the stages of early object relationships. Abraham's conception of these stages, while taking aggression very much into account, was also correlated with the stages of psychosexual development on which Freud had remained focused for the most part. Thus, Klein's pioneering efforts and her creativity led the way to expanding the theory of envy. It freed envy from the necessarily triangular and primarily libidinal emphasis that expressed Freud's commitment to the Darwinism of his day.

Of special importance is Klein's degendering envy by focusing mainly on its roots for both sexes in the early child–mother relationship. Envy is a factor to be reckoned with from the first stages of development. However, her bold, if not extravagant, speculations about envy's having constitutional origins seem to have been pretty much left by the wayside. Spillius (1993) has provided an excellent general review of the history of envy in Kleinian thought.

Some of the differences between Freud and Klein originated in their different approaches to the place of object relations in development. Freud's focus on the instinctual drives led him to link object relations to these drives as one of their manifestations (Freud 1915c). Instincts, he said there, are object seeking. According to Freud (1920), a pair of quasibiological instincts dominates life: a Life Instinct and a Death Instinct. Although Klein followed Freud faithfully respect to those two instincts, she also posited that object relations exist from the beginning stages of life and so might be used as the framework for describing their development and manifestations.

As Klein's ideas underwent development, these object relations were not portrayed as fully developed representations, the infant not yet being capable of the level of thinking on which relationships as understood in maturity can be conceived. Rather, object relations are first experienced as primordial pleasure–pain reactions and somatic reactions, and it is these that are the foundation stones of later feelings and fantasies about relations with others (Isaacs 1948).

The infant exists in what Klein (1946) named the paranoid-schizoid position. Only with the attainment of the more mature depressive position, with its ascendance of libidinal over hostile and destructive factors, is it possible to have and maintain stable, responsible, loving relations with whole objects in life as well as unconscious fantasy (Klein 1940). In one way, Klein was following Freud by viewing the earliest paranoid-schizoid phases of object relatedness as not only narcissistic but also strongly hostile and fearful. Freud had described them that way in "Mourning and Melancholia" (1917) and "Instincts and Their Vicissitudes" (1915c).

In "Envy and Gratitude," Klein (1957) centered more attention on envy than on gratitude, although defenses against gratitude did receive some attention. I believe that imbalance expressed her constant attention to the damage that envy can inflict on the psychoanalytic process—most likely the same damage that it has inflicted on the analysand's psychic development in general. Also, by focusing on the paranoid-schizoid aspects of her analysands' functioning, she highlighted their aggressive, narcissistic tendencies, among which envy figures prominently.

Klein did not propose that one ever totally overcomes the substructure of the paranoid-schizoid envy. Consequently, her theory states that human beings are bound to respond ambivalently to the goodness of others and that it is a life's work for each human being to come to terms with this ambivalence, to limit its destructive potential and mitigate its often subtle forms of destructiveness.

Clinically, then, it is inevitable that envy will be stimulated by the goodness of the caregiving analyst trying to understand in order to be helpful. During analysis, the analyst must be alert for signs of envy every step of the way.

THE DIFFERENCE IN *WELTANSCHAUUNG*

To return to one of the main differences between Klein and Freud in the context of envy—the centrality of fantasized object relations in understanding the dynamics of the internal world—it seems correct to say that *Klein was theorizing from a basically different outlook on the problems of existence.* Although Freud (1933) argued—correctly, I believe—that psychoanalysis does not provide a basis for any *Weltanschauung*, it seems that he did not take into account the ways in which theorists' values are necessarily expressed in the kind of theorizing they develop and the kind of practice associated with this theorizing. By *Weltanschauung* Freud had in mind only a conscious systematic ethics or set of values one uses to guide her or his conduct in life. In contrast, contemporary critical theorists assume that *Weltanschauungen* codetermine all aspects of one's mode of theorizing about human existence. One's general outlook sets the terms of theoretical discussion and the questions to be addressed. We see that this was so in Freud's thinking about the psychical consequences of the anatomical distinction between the sexes. To my knowledge, Klein did not take up this question explicitly; however, it can be inferred from her way of thinking about psychoanalysis.

Thus, impersonalized drivenness is one way—Freud's way—to thematize human development; Klein's primordial human relatedness is another. For Freud, relatedness was a means to an end; for Klein, relatedness was at the center of what it is all about from beginning to end. Envy disrupts relatedness or, put otherwise, steers it toward destructiveness. Many other aspects of Klein's theorizing are the same as or similar to Freud's, both of them having invested constitutional givens with significant influence on psychical development; both positioned conflict or ambivalence at the center of their dynamic formulations; they attached therapeutic importance to reconstructions of early infantile experience; and, perhaps most important, they worked extensively with the dual instinct theory. Klein's fuller and more inclusive rendition of envy stands on this common foundation. In Freud's developmental theory, envy remained primarily a vicissitude of gender identity and its effect on self-esteem; for Klein, envy was a pervasive existential given. Different outlooks on life, different theories, and different technical consequences.

CLINICAL CONSIDERATIONS

There is a story told of Wilfred Bion's having said to a group member who had been attacking him at a Tavistock group relations conference, "I can't see why you hate me; I haven't tried to help you." Here, following Klein, Bion was indicating that we might think of envy in the transference as well as in relationships in general as a case of biting the hand that feeds you. What you envy is the other's possession of some goodness that you believe you lack. Along with goodness, you might envy control, power to frustrate by withholding, and in analysis, the analyst's peace of mind, sanity, and benevolence. Analysands envy these qualities because, being in a conflictual state of need, they are likely to feel, on the one hand, rendered vulnerable or helpless by their strong dependent, greedy feelings, and on the other, enraged, humiliated, and increasingly turned toward fantasies of total, omnipotent self-sufficiency. In this simultaneously exalted, debased, and otherwise defensive position, they envy and wish to attack, spoil, or eliminate their analysts' goodness or any other experienced differences between them (Frankiel 2000).

Unconsciously, this spoiling attack is accomplished by projecting one's hateful feelings into the envied other; then the other becomes a poisonous breast or a threatening hand rather than a full or generous one. Alternatively, the envious person may project her or his own state of humiliation in order to devalue the other, eliminate the felt difference, and so eliminate the stimulus to envy. In either case, the attacking person might also feel guilty and unworthy for generating these fantasies and behaviors, and as a result she or he will envy the other's goodness all the more. In the end, the envious person gets caught up in a vicious circle in which biting the hand that feeds you becomes a guilty way of life or perhaps a life threatened by persecutory, retaliatory others. The aggressiveness concealed by that guilty or frightened way of life might be further disguised by being sugarcoated with idealizations. Here, I am referring to a painfully familiar clinical phenomenon: we analysts being covered with psychical bites and band-aids. To say that our analysands keep us in stitches is not to refer to laughing matters.

Klein (1957) advanced the idea that it is this vicious circle that is the basis of those severe negative therapeutic reactions that block or reverse analytic advances and, by stimulating negative countertransference, undermine the analyst's analytic attitude. Before "Envy and Gratitude" appeared, Joan Riviere (1936) had already written a classic paper on the negative therapeutic reaction. Riviere had based her interpretation on Klein's (1935) early approach to formulating the depressive position. Specifically, Riviere had detailed the analysand's fear of advancing developmentally into a position in which intolerable guilt would be felt were it not promptly cancelled by regression. Riviere added immeasurably to Freud's (1923) major but narrower oedipal understanding of the guilt factor in the negative therapeutic reaction (see, however, Chapter 8 for a critique of this "negative" conception of these events).

So far, so good, but it remained for Klein to make the great leap forward to defining the central role of envious transference in the negative therapeutic reaction. Consequently, we must always sort out when our analysands are suffering from our lapses, when from their own painful internal or external situations, and when from the benefits of our very best efforts. Keeping in mind the last of these possibilities spares us many moments of intense negative countertransference.

I believe that envy figures in the so-called negative therapeutic reaction in other ways as well. For one, there is anxiety in response to the fantasy of the envious analyst. This fantasy is not rare among analysands when they report achievements at work and gratifications in love. Guiltily, the analysand might feel that he or she has surpassed the analyst by stealing the analyst's goodness, leaving behind only an empty shell—a sick, crippled, depleted, castrated figure. Aspects of this fantasy are often discernible before vacation periods and termination. Then, it may be implied in ideas that the analyst, desperate for relief, replenishment, and escape from further abuse, is only too glad to get away, stay away, or finish up once and for all. The analysand is engaging in self-blame throughout, just as a rejected or abandoned child might do, with some fear of retaliation most likely playing its part, too.

The analysand might also fear being envied on other scores, such as youth, good looks, wealth, worldly power, and time for second chances (when that is the case). Much of this envy is likely to be the result of secondary projective identification, by which I mean that the analysand finds embodied in the analyst the envious mother and father who have already been constructed to a significant extent on the basis of projective identifications that have intensified actual parental characteristics and behavior. There is no denying that some parents are pathologically envious. There are many such, and they can lay waste to their children's freedom to develop and use their own assets.

Also to be taken into account in this context is the envy felt by others in the environment toward the progressed analysand. Klein pointed out how much envy is stimulated in everyday life by one's appearing to have genuinely mastered (come to terms with) ambivalence, strengthened one's integration, and become relatively unburdened by the sadism, masochism, and envy with which the average person is still struggling. These envious others—often close friends and relatives—are quick to be challenging, disparaging, or ostracizing. As a result, the social price of mature integration can get to seem too high. Becoming discouraged and feeling deprived, the analysand then regresses time and time again. Momentarily, the sense of being persecuted by friends, lovers, family, colleagues, and the community at large might seem to be diminished by defensive regression; however, regression is soon followed by acutely painful feelings of loss, defeat, despair, resentment, and a renewed basis for an envious outlook on others. At the same time, the analyst does well to remember that projective identification of envious internal figures may well have been magnifying the appearance that others react only or mainly with envy. Envious superego figures are especially likely to be projected (Britton 2001, Frankiel 2001, O'Shaughnessy 1999).

Mention must be made of yet another constituent of envious contexts: the analysand's *defenses against envy*, some aspects of which have already been mentioned. Melanie Klein attended to this factor carefully. The analysand attempts to hide envy by playing the part of the unobjectionable good patient: responsive, grateful, thoughtful, and so on. Splitting and idealization facilitate his or her playing this defensive role. The analysand aims to ward off envy's narcissistic aggressiveness and the persecutory anxiety it stimulates. This defense, with its cover of modesty or unassumingness, also obscures persisting unconscious fantasies of omnipotence that both contribute to envy of difference and compensate for the reactive sense of lack or defect it evokes.

One encounters this configuration in some analysands with strong pseudonormal defenses. Notoriously difficult to analyze deeply owing to the rapidity with which they experience the analyst's probing efforts as both unappreciative and persecutory, they betray no trace of envy, indeed no need to be envious. In this defensive posture, the development and creative use of their personal capacities are likely to be seriously hampered by being deployed narrowly in the service of appearances and a basically fragile sense of sanity.

COUNTERTRANSFERENCE

Melanie Klein did not contribute much to developing the prominent place now occupied by countertransference in the work of contemporary Kleinians (Spillius 1993). Paula Heimann (1950) opened up this box. Here, I want to emphasize some additional supplementary ideas on envy. For one thing, the analyst might actually envy the analysand for reasons of the sort I mentioned earlier: health, wealth, youth, power, talent, and so on. Additionally, the envious analyst might fall back on projective identification of envious feelings and then too readily attribute envy to the analysand or at least too readily center on envy that is discernible but perhaps not to the point at that time. Analysts have acknowledged envying their analysands when, proud of their advanced ways of analyzing, they regard their analysands as getting better analyses than they did. In this, they are much like some envious "too good" parents. Obviously, the envious analyst will find it difficult to intervene in ways that are empathic, accurate, balanced, and therefore effective.

Another countertransferential hazard is analysts' acceptance and enjoyment of the defensive idealizations their analysands use to mask their own envy. These analysts may then feel truly enviable in possessing all the virtues of unblemished tact, sensitivity, deep understanding, and extreme helpfulness. On the other hand, as Heinz Kohut (1977) emphasized, the analyst might respond to being idealized by becoming anxious and defensively humble, owing to the threat of her or his latent grandiosity being stimulated too strongly. To this factor we may add that, as a result, the analyst might become blind to the analysand's struggle with envy in the transference. In these cases, even when self-satisfaction might accompany what seems like a good piece of analytic work, the analyst will find it difficult to enjoy and hang on to that experience.

The biggest hazard that I have noted in my work as analyst and supervisor lies in the analyst's doubts about his or her own goodness as a person and analyst. We analysts all experience these doubts, some of us more often and more severely than others. These doubts are there to be played on by the envious analysand, that is, the analysand who is intent on spoiling the experience of rendering good analytic care and understanding that is in keeping with our work ideals and humanistic values. In this context, either spontaneously or reactively, we can lose sight of our reparative goodness and lose the poise and confidence necessary to discern and take up calmly the analysand's envy and projected envy. On account of these inner doubts, we can be too ready to focus on our own self-esteem problems and the irritable state we find ourselves in.

Melanie Klein would say that, here, much depends on the analyst's having advanced far in his or her development toward the ideal: the depressive position. Then, the analyst would be able, in a relatively stable way, to accept and regulate inevitable tendencies toward ambivalence. The analyst will continue to believe not only in her or his goodness but also in the power of unconscious fantasy and primitive defenses to block or impair its being experienced as such, however imperfect it may be and however mixed with aggressive potential. I emphasize *imperfect* goodness because it is our lot to live with ambivalence that we never overcome totally. In Freud's terms, it is, as usual, the quantitative factor, not the qualitative, that will probably make the big difference in the conclusions one draws. When it comes to the problems associated with envy and gratitude, the quantitative factor is likely to be the decisive one.

A discussion of envy cannot end without mention of admiration. Admiration should not be minimized by being subsumed under gratitude. Strongly felt and freely expressed admiration signifies some security in maintaining to a sufficient degree the depressive position. The existence of Melanie Klein's great classic, "Envy and Gratitude" deserves our admiration as well as our gratitude, and, to be true to Klein, we must expect that admiration to be tinged with envy as well.

CHAPTER 5

THE PSYCHOTHERAPIST'S ABSENCE

In this chapter, I will broaden the coverage of method to include all psychoanalytically oriented treatment. This is not to imply that what has come before or what will come later is not broadly applicable, too, but only that in the other chapters I have tried to stay clear and focused by referring to the psychoanalytic process alone.

It is to be expected that patients will center transference feelings on their psychotherapists' many different features: appearance, professional manner, routine, office setting, speech patterns, and so on. They will also single out the content of what their psychotherapists say, its variations and frequency, and the attitude these communications seem to convey. Especially prominent among the multitude of psychotherapist variables are the psychotherapists' absences. *Absence* is the aspect I have chosen to explore in this chapter. I will describe how the analysis of absence, both physical and emotional and both actual and imagined, can open up key issues in the patient's disturbed and disturbing unconscious fantasies of relations with others. Further insight will be gained into major sources of anxiety, guilt, shame, and envy. Additionally, there will be much examination of exaggerated flux in self-esteem and self-cohesion, sexual and aggressive arousal and activity, means and effectiveness of coping with loss, and the ambivalence surrounding emotional dependency.

Also, I will examine the idea of absence itself, especially because there is reason to think that, in the instance of any therapeutic relationship, the idea of *total* absence does not survive close scrutiny. Even when the analytic process is ending and the participants discontinue their meetings, the impact of the physical absence that follows is not correctly described as an experience of total absence. My analysis of absence will rest on taking into account interpretations of unconscious and sometimes conscious fantasies of relations with others, with all their conceptually concrete features and all their influence on daily life from the time of early development.

As I develop this position, it should become clear that it has important consequences for the interpretation of the ways in which patients experience any absence and how they then respond to it. My discussion will include technical suggestions and remarks on countertransference and enactment: *countertransference* both in psychotherapists' feelings about being away from their distressed patients and in those moments of psychical or emotional absence that counteract whatever rapport they have established with their patients, and *enactment* when psychotherapists realize that they have been acting *toward* their patients or *with* them in ways that play into, and even stimulate or validate, their patients' pathological fantasies.

THE EXPERIENCE OF ABSENCE

Patients can experience their psychotherapists as being absent even though physically they are unmistakably

present. Often, these "absences" are imagined, the psychotherapists being in their usual listening mode. Then, the
experiences of absence frequently express projections of
the patients' own withdrawn, withholding, or rejecting
states. For example, there is the not-rare patient who ac-
cuses the therapist of never saying anything when that is
far from the case and when it is closer to the truth that, for
whatever reason, the patient cannot register what is being
offered in the way of clarification and interpretation. In
some instances, the patient's feeling burdened by the
therapist's alleged silence may stem from unacknowledged
conscious withholding on the patient's part, the theme
then being not *who* but rather *what* withholding is taking
place.

Sometimes, however, this charge of silence may stem
from the therapist's addressing the patient on the wrong
level of mental functioning, perhaps being too abstract or
complex or perhaps bringing up content for which the patient is not ready. Then, "you never say anything" might
mean "anything I can use or tolerate" or "anything I can
integrate into my sense of myself." In this instance, the
patient's charge might be taken as a useful form of supervision. Even so, the psychotherapist does best to regard
the patient's particular experience of absence as having
been jointly produced, for the patient's unconscious fantasy will have played its influential part in shaping the experience of that absence and its overt expression. For instance, the therapist who has been on the wrong level
might acknowledge the legitimate aspects of the patient's
grievance ("I guess you felt I loaded too much on you all at
once," or "I realize I wasn't quite in tune with you then")
and also point out that, significantly, the patient has experienced the temporary difficulty in communication as *total*
or *chronic* unresponsiveness, an unresponsiveness equiva-

lent to total silence and in that sense total absence. Addressing this accusation might then open up issues of negativism, disappointment, or despair.

Sometimes, the patient might experience the psychotherapist as absent upon correctly perceiving that he or she *is* withdrawn, unresponsive, or inattentive, so much so that the patient feels alone, helpless, and abandoned. In addition to self-analysis, the psychotherapist does best not to neglect the possibility that the patient's emotional position has somehow contributed to this occurrence, as might be the case when a defensive patient plays it safe by hiding behind extreme circumstantiality; if so, the therapist might look for a propitious moment and a tactful way to take up this deadening influence on the relationship.

At other times the patient might refer to absence only obliquely, as, for example, by mentioning not feeling "together." In this instance, the patient might be using a transformation of self-experience to communicate a sense that it is the two of them who are not together, that is, out of contact emotionally—further, that he or she needs that emotional contact to feel "together" but does not experience the psychotherapist as doing his or her part.

The therapist's psychical absence, real or imagined, is usually experienced painfully, sometimes more painfully than all those physical absences that take place between appointments, over weekends, and during cancellations, holidays, and vacation times. However that may be, it is usually a good idea to at least call attention to the experience of absence, try to explore it, and if possible interpret its emotional tone and fantasy content, because ignoring intimations of loss of contact is known to be conducive to disruptive acting out. This acting out often takes the form of the patient's adopting a retaliatory stance that is expressed through absences, lateness, silences, and perhaps even breaking off the treatment. It is likely that these retaliatory responses include masochistic elements in that, ultimately, it is the patient who is almost certain to be the loser. More obviously masochistic are reactive, self-injurious social and physical actions which, when reported after the therapist's disturbing absence, are conveyed in ways intended to provoke the psychotherapist's guilt and so warrant being labeled sadomasochistic transference reactions.

Also to be included here are those patients who characteristically turn on themselves, blaming themselves for the therapist's absences, citing how they are boring, difficult, unlovable, uncomprehending, ungrateful, and altogether undeserving. In this way they also protect their defensive idealization of the therapist as the one who presumably will single-handedly save them from themselves. Nevertheless, one finds in all these instances considerable disappointment, feelings of betrayal and humiliation, and hateful and envious attitudes from which, so the patient feels, the therapist must be protected by being kept out of range through idealization.

The patient's painful experience of absence should not be thought of as based only on feelings of deprivation and derogation. In many instances, jealousy plays a key role. In this respect it is a question of where the patient imagines the therapist to be when he or she is away physically or mentally. There are two groups of fantasies that I consider the ones most commonly encountered. One group centers on primal scene fantasies, specifically, fantasies of the psychotherapist as sexually engaged with someone else. In these primal scenes, the sexual acts may be tender, sadomasochistic, or otherwise what is conventionally (and in my opinion pejoratively) called perverse (Schafer

1997a). In this instance, the jealousy might be expressing the patient's own sexual desire for the psychotherapist or the therapist's mate, or a wish to be included in a triangular primal scene, a prospect that is both exciting and frightening.

The second set of jealous fantasies centers on the psychotherapist as a parental figure being more devoted and more giving to others in his or her care, as if too busy with siblings or new babies to keep the patient in mind. One common prototype of this transference reaction is the mother nursing the next baby. In these instances, the patient's fantasy is dyadic rather than triadic and stems from preoedipal transference feelings. Both family configurations may be implied, either in condensation or more or less rapid alternation.

Sometimes, envy contributes additional intensity to the pains of absence. This is so, for example, when the patient feels that the therapist is free to come and go, whereas she or he must stick to the regular schedule and be responsive; or the therapist is free to talk or not, in contrast to the patient, who is expected to keep talking. In this connection, the patient's sense of self-worth or dignity is felt to be diminished by the therapist's greater autonomy; however, behind this deflating experience of the relationship may lie unconscious fantasies of omnipotence that maintain inflated self-regard. Unconsciously, envy of the therapist is likely to be an all-or-none matter. Consciously, however, and empathetically, the envious patient might represent it as simply a matter of fairness: equality, mutuality, or absence of hierarchic distributions of power.

As discussed in Chapter 4, the implied envy might be directed elsewhere, for instance, onto the psychotherapist's effective self-interest, self-respect, sanity, benevolence, and general self-enhancement. Then, the patient's reactive selfhurtfulness and grievances might include efforts to bring down the therapist, to shatter his or her pride in the treatment and pride in the self as a dedicated professional healer. By taking this envious course of spoiling, the patient might also be defending against fantasies, already described in Chapter 3, of being left behind as a dirty, worthless piece of excrement, puddle of vomit, or greedy, insatiable mouth or monster.

THE IDEA OF ABSENCE

It is generally agreed that understanding the vicissitudes of the therapeutic relationship requires a steady focus on shifting signs of transference. Since Freud's earliest expositions, therapeutic thinking about transference has been guided by one essential but typically tacit assumption. I will try to make that assumption explicit and develop some of its implications, not so much with the hope of adding something new as with the aim of adding to the effectiveness of interpretation. My discussion centers on concrete thinking, for interpretations often become more precise and effective when they are appropriately close to concrete, primitive modes of unconscious function.

The assumption I refer to is this. In unconscious fantasy, the figure of the psychotherapist is a constant. The psychotherapist is always present. This means that the sense of relationship between the two participants is continuous even if, consciously, not always equally active or prominent. Sometimes, this continuous object relationship takes the form of identification with the therapist, identification being a well-known means of undoing separation and object loss. Sometimes, however, other figures may be substituted for one or both of the therapeutic participants, this operation effected by displacements of the sort encountered in dream interpretation. Consequently, it is not presence but rather the experience of absence that must be regarded as the significant variable. This variable complicates but does not contradict the continuity of the transference.

The experience of absence is to be regarded either as conscious material to be treated like any other manifest content (though often of a more important kind), or as having been absorbed into unconscious fantasy as a seemingly paradoxical element. In the latter instance, a psychotherapist is created who is both present and absent. I will soon review some of the ways in which this seeming paradox of simultaneous presence and absence may be represented. First, however, more must be said about the consequences of this assumption that, once unconscious fantasy is taken into account, presence is the constant and experience of absence is the variable.

What is entailed by the assumption that the therapist remains a constant reference point for the patient and often may be safely described as such in interpretations? Even when the patient seems to be talking only about matters other than the therapy itself, even matters of great moment, there is implied a particular stance toward the psychotherapist, an attitude or a set of expectations that shapes what is being told, how it is told, and when and why. In this respect the therapist assumes that, at every moment, there is a plenitude of things to talk about and that there are many times, ways, and reasons to choose a topic, adopt a slant on it, and select the words for it. Consequently it is often more important that the therapist attend to these details rather than to the literal content being conveyed by the patient. These details are more likely to indicate important transference fantasies and feelings and thereby open the way into available emotional intensity in the here-and-now clinical situation. Often, the key to unlocking the transference fantasy is paying close attention to any sign of added defensiveness or other shifts in the patient's emotional posture at the moment: restlessness, throatiness of speech, edgy or cold tone of voice, abrupt silence—whatever. Until the patient's change of delivery or manner has been brought into focus and explored, the immediate content might not retain, attain, or regain its value for the therapy.

To work in this manner is not to brush aside the importance of emotionally loaded life material. It is just that this manifest life material might parallel the latent transference while being used to keep away from open and threatening reference to it. This material is to be respected as significant and yet, in its manifest aspect, not to the point at that moment. At times, the psychotherapist must make a judgment call and so might act in a way that proves to be off the mark, tactless, provocative, or mechanical; surprisingly often, however, this alternative to taking important life material at face value turns out to profit the therapy. The therapist assumes that effective transference interpretation furthers the patient's psychic integration and puts her or him in the best position to deal with the weighty life material the direct discussion of which has been deferred. As Loewald (1960) put it, one aims ultimately to bring the patient to a higher, more effective level of psychic function, and one does so by interpreting.

I should emphasize at this point that I am not recommending an either/or attitude in this regard. I believe that the psychotherapist does best not to rush past significant life content; preferably, the therapist hovers close to a balance between staying with the patient's life topics and finding ways to introduce significant and timely implica-

77

tions of transference. The thing is not to get very involved in interpreting content that seems to have no bearing on the transference of the moment.

Returning to the seeming paradox of simultaneous presence and absence, this simultaneity may be expressed in several different ways. In one way, the conception of the psychotherapist might be split, there then being in unconscious fantasy a psychotherapist who, for example, is concerned and interested, and another psychotherapist, perhaps a rigid technician, who is scornful of the "superficial material" on which the patient is dwelling. It will be the allegedly rigid, part-object therapist who is psychically absent to the patient; the other therapist is present, perhaps too present for comfort. In one case a split of this kind was attached to an idea that one part of the split represented the patient's warm, caring father figure and the other her cold, distant mother figure; among other things, this split indicated failed integration or coordination of identifications. Simultaneity is being expressed in another way when the patient complains, implores, or coaxes an emotionally absent therapist, real or imagined, to be more attentive or more responsive; here there is a psychotherapist who, though experienced as absent, is sufficiently present to be appealed to. In yet another way, when the psychotherapist is physically absent, the patient might experience him or her as present: present nearby as a "presence" (Schafer 1968) or present in the internal world, perhaps as a critical voice, perhaps as a supportive guide or observer.

Consider in this regard the case of the psychotherapist who will soon be physically absent from the therapy, say, on vacation, or who has just returned from being away and is confronted by a vociferously protesting or acting-out patient. It is often useful to understand this patient as attempting to limit both the therapist's thinking and also his or her own thinking. By setting this limit, by focusing so sharply on external physical matters alone, the patient could well be attempting to exclude interpretation of unconscious fantasies of presence.

Whatever other meaning these protests may have or whatever other purposes they may serve, these reactions to absence are understandable as defensive moves: unconsciously, the patient is aiming to block any recognition of what has happened or is happening to the therapeutic relationship in her or his internal world. Has the internalized therapist's attitude toward the patient been transformed from positive to negative? Has the therapist been split, the good part repressed and the bad, abandoning part highlighted? In unconscious fantasy, the patient might very well be equating repression of the good part with a totally destructive attack on him or her and be feeling guilty or afraid of reprisals. When this is the case, the patient's noisy grievances against the therapist for having been away can divert attention from the patient's own abandoning or destructive fantasies. Then, it is a case of offense being the best defense. The destroyed, destructive, frightened, or guilt-bearing party is being made out to be the other, that is, the therapist.

Simultaneity also plays a part in the internal world of the patient who does not see why it should make a difference whether or not the therapist is present over weekends, during holidays, or between sessions. This is the patient—not a rare one either—who declares that the therapeutic sessions are only small fragments of long days filled with serious matters and that it is best not to regard them otherwise. Persisting with this literal-minded, seemingly pragmatic, conscious account sometimes amounts to a virtually impregnable defense against therapy as a manifestation of transference and against other transference tendencies. The therapist might then be limited to pointing out repeatedly, when this is so, and over a long period of time how regularly it may be observed that disruptions of function and mood coincide with her or his comings and goings. This patient might finally agree, even if only intellectually, that there does seem to be reason to consider that absences do make a difference, or perhaps that the absent therapist has somehow remained a disturbing presence while physically absent. Some limited access to transference fantasies might be gained this way. Better some than none. The example of Ted, introduced in Chapter 1 and taken up again in other chapters, is a case in point.

In some instances, however, the psychotherapist must finally fall back on trying to do as much therapy as possible away from the transference, and hope, not unreasonably, that the patient's increased psychological mindedness, if any, will be carried over into some insight into the therapeutic relationship. Although it is tempting to think that this apparently unmoved patient might have a very weak capacity to develop attachments to others, it can be more useful to assume that he or she is constantly and effectively blocking a strong desire for overt relationships, maintaining lively unconscious fantasies of relatedness, but blocking incorporation of the therapist's insights (Schafer 1997a). Consequently, these interventions are best touched on lightly, as though in passing or parenthetically; alternatively, they might be held in reserve, often for extended periods of time. In neither case should they be regarded as an attempt to bypass defense or ignore transference but rather as an attempt to be present enough in the therapeutic situation for the patient to make what use he or she can make of the therapist, perhaps even appropriating insights and claiming them later as independent achievements. Sometimes, what matters to these patients is not so much attachment to others as sensitivity to their doings, for they, particularly the most narcissistic of them, depend on the responses of others to maintain their own precarious sense of omnipotence and self-worth.

There are times when, on the basis of projective identification, the physically absent psychotherapist is imagined to have been driven into retaliatory departure by resentment of the patient. At other times, the therapist has been forced to be "abandoning" so that he or she knows through direct experience something of the patient's own bitter life of feeling excluded. In both instances, interpretation must focus on projective identification.

In another variation, and as will be discussed more fully in the next chapter, denial of one's own goodness might play an important part in the response to absence. It is likely that this denial is being used in part to stave off feelings of concern for the therapist's well-being and general morale while the two are apart. Behind the patient's conscious attitude of indifference, there may lie intense, ambivalence-based anxiety about the therapist's health or safety, his or her interest in returning to the patient, or the ability to do so. Certainly these worries might reflect reaction formation against hostile feelings toward the psychotherapist rather than denial of goodness; however, they also come up when there has been a turn in the therapy toward the patient's beginning to accept and feel concern for the psychotherapist as a whole person and to dread the excitement and potential disappointment and pain that that experience entails.

Projective identification plays its part in another response to absence. The patient complains that the therapist does not, has not, or will not think about the patient at all during the time the two are apart, when it is the patient who finds it difficult to maintain any image of the therapist during his or her absence. Unconsciously, that image may have been destroyed in anger or abandoned, though consciously it may be experienced only as slipping away or fading. One patient reported that she had to be sure I thought about her while I was away so that she could feel alive or feel that she really existed. To this end, she often acted out in a way that created crises in her life just before I went away, hoping that as a result I would be worrying about her during the separation. The positive aspect of her acknowledging this stratagem was its expressing confidence in me; for before then, she had been leading an emotionally isolated life, though one outwardly very much wrapped up in social relationships. Earlier, she would have been more likely to project into me indifferent narcissism or punitive rejection, and she would not have sought to feel that she was still with me during my absences.

Sometimes problems of this sort are best defined as the patient's being unable, during separations, to independently maintain a supportive or positive attitude toward the self, and, as a result, having to rely on the therapist's presence or interest to feel at all secure and stable. Then, physical absence leaves the patient feeling exposed to merciless attacks on the self from an envious, self-destructive set of superego imperatives. Yet, here too it is useful to think of the allegedly absent therapist as being present in one or another role: critic, indifferent observer, or passively aggressive bystander withholding the necessary support, unwilling to serve as a bulwark against attacks on the self, and in general acting like an indifferent god contemplating the persecution of a helpless mortal.

In the course of therapy one often sees these seemingly paradoxical condensations of representations of the psychotherapist. Absence might not even appear as such. A dream or fantasy might feature, for example, a male therapist who has literally turned his back on the patient or a female therapist who, looking older, weaker, smaller, is disappearing.

Condensation of contradictory characteristics did not go unnoticed by Freud. For example, in *Totem and Taboo* (1912c), Freud used anthropological as well as psychotherapeutic material to note how often the dead remain quite alive: observing, judging, protecting, or punishing. In this, they are, so to say, the living dead, in which case both deadness and aliveness are simultaneously affirmed. It is not even a case of negation as a halfway measure of the sort described by Freud (1927). In just the same way, as I have already noted, the physically absent therapist can be present to the patient so that, for better or worse, the patient will later report, "You were with me."

Whether or not the figure of the absent therapist is split or condensed, the therapist is obliged to remember her or his unconsciously maintained continuous presence and so to refrain from taking at face value the patient's claims of simply having been abandoned or left behind. In this type of situation, if anyone gets left behind it is the therapist who, in desperate defense or destructive retaliation, has been put out of mind.

This way of coping by patients is not at all the same as that of the more or less balanced psychotherapist on vacation who has put thoughts about the patient on hold until his or her return to the treatment. Technically, the key questions are for the patient to answer rather than the therapist; specifically, "Where were *you* and what were *you* doing during this absence?" And "In what state were *you* imagining *me*?" Then, the interpretation, "You felt me to be not with you because you got rid of me; that was your retaliation" or "It would have been too humiliating to you to think of me because it would mean you missed me," or "You devalued me so much that I no longer seemed to have anything of value to offer, so why care about my being away?!"

Another manifestation of seemingly paradoxical condensation is evident in the following instance: the therapist is away on vacation and it seems that the patient is unconsciously imagining him or her to have been worn out and depleted by the work and so has had to leave for a period of recuperation and restoration. However, the therapist lingers in the patient's fantasies not only as a damaged figure but as a dangerously persecutory figure as well, one who will retaliate destructively for having been thus impaired.

In these instances it is not helpful to conceptualize the figure of the psychotherapist as split into two different types of being, for doing so is too likely to signify to the patient that the psychotherapist is retreating into everyday rationality, that is, away from the unconscious modes of mental function. Preferably, the interpretation should present the therapist as a compound figure, both weakened and so hardly present and frighteningly strong and so overwhelmingly present. The therapy of these compound figures is often seriously complicated by the patient's own layered defenses not only against these negative ways of experiencing the therapist but also against the primitive modes of experience that produce paradoxical figures of this sort. The therapist's retreat from this level of comprehension reinforces the patient's insecurity and defensiveness.

COUNTERTRANSFERENCE

Absence of whatever sort causes problems, not only for the patient but for the therapist as well. However, in view of the assumption of continuous presence in unconscious fantasy, it becomes especially important to approach countertransference first in a more general way. For now one must begin by asking whether and to what extent it must follow that the patient is continuously present in *the psychotherapist's unconscious fantasies*. If it were just a matter of logic, one could easily say that it is safe to assume that what goes for one goes for the other. However, saying, as I did a short while back, that the patient has been put on hold during the therapist's actual absence can still imply this presence without suggesting that it is in the forefront of the therapist's concerns. Indeed, some of the current advocates of the intersubjective-interpersonalist approach seem to have included this further assumption in what I regard as their highly ideological emphasis on transforming what they call the traditionally elitist and unreal therapeutic relationship into an egalitarian one in which, equally, both participants are to disclose important fantasies and intense feelings.

In principle, a firm believer in the continuing power of infantile unconscious fantasy cannot accept this egalitarian emphasis. For the psychotherapist, the therapeutic relationship remains tilted, regardless of her or his intentions; the patient's transference sees to that. Although these differences usually diminish as therapy takes effect, they, like those concerning one's parents, are never completely eliminated. The most useful conception of the therapeutic situation is that it requires specialization of function based on different degrees of subjective distress and different degrees of preparation for understanding the workings of unconscious fantasy. The consequences for the two participants in functioning and emotion should be different both qualitatively and quantitatively.

The place of the patient in the psychotherapist's unconscious fantasies is worth considering further. Optimally, that place is not large outside the therapeutic sessions and its role is not predominant. Certainly, in emergencies there is much to warrant concerned, conscious preoccupation. In these cases there is bound to be some arousal of unconscious fantasies of rescue and punishment and feelings of rage and shame as well as excitement, all of which calls for some self-therapy or consultation with colleagues, perhaps even a period of supervision, especially when the therapist's feelings seem to be getting out of hand. Ordinarily, however, the psychotherapist whose life is reasonably stable is not likely to be so intensely invested in any one patient or in all of them that other interests, concerns, and pleasures fall by the wayside or get shifted into the shadows. There is, however, special reason for alertness when termination of the therapy approaches, all the more so when the therapy has been prolonged, for then the therapist's own feelings of loss, and intellectual defenses against them, are likely to put in their appearance in ways both obvious and subtle.

At this point, mention must be made of other aspects of countertransference, specifically, those expressed by the therapist's psychical absence. The patient is likely to sense this absence and then, in fantasy, unconsciously elaborate and exaggerate it. Although it may be that these withdrawals into inattentiveness or boredom, sometimes even apathy, have been stimulated by the patient's conduct in the treatment, there is much else to weigh: circumstances in the psychotherapist's life can impair him or her as an empathic, attentive, and intelligent listener and interpreter. These circumstances include births, deaths, illnesses, lack of sleep, and professional emergencies. Psychical absence can be a defensive response to the material being considered. Occasional absences of this type may be easy to analyze; analyzing their deeper aspects takes longer.

Recurrent *psychical* absence is another matter. It calls at least for intensive consultation or more treatment of the therapist. There are too many factors—relational and psychopathological—to list and discuss here. To mention just a few of its manifestations, however, psychical absence often takes the form of a mechanical approach or a preference for supportive and controlling methods. Perhaps a defensive medication-minded therapeutic approach will be used prematurely or unnecessarily. These manifestations may be mainly a matter of conformity to collegial or HMO pressures or legal self-protection, but behind them may lie some obsessional trends perhaps mixed with such paranoid-schizoid, narcissistic features as excessive need for control, fantasies of omnipotence, and denial of the internal world.

Another type of countertransference problem becomes plain when the psychotherapist begins to feel undue anxiety and guilt about being physically away from patients, perhaps worrying that they should not have been left "alone" in their painful states, even when adequate coverage has been arranged. It is not easy to mark off where appropriate concern ends and undue anxiety and guilt begin, but there are obvious extremes that can lead unconsciously to questionable extra appointments, unusual and burdensome extensions of the length of therapeutic sessions and even of the entire therapy, constant telephone calls, and so on. In these instances, the significant parts may be played by unempathic projective identifications in both directions. Then what takes place is more in the nature of enactment than enabling participation in the therapy—enactment that may perpetuate and even exaggerate both the patient's and the therapist's distress.

The psychotherapist's own characterological countertransference (Reich 1951) may play a part here, and it is that to which the patient's projective identifications will attach themselves as to a neurological receptor site. In this regard, I single out the almost ubiquitous need to be in the role of the caring, helping, and understanding person who enters into the career choice of therapist. A psychotherapist who goes to extremes in this respect might be projecting into the patient excessive concern about absence and so make absence much more of an issue than can be attributed simply to the patient's projections and other manipulations. Here, as elsewhere, it is best not to jump to conclusions, but rather to allow time for adequate reflection and observation. Circumstances do often dictate quick decisions, however; then, one must do the best one can.

THE EXPERIENCE OF PRESENCE

This chapter would be incomplete without some discussion of the psychotherapist's presence. When one considers all the benefits of reliable physical and psychical presence, it seems at first that absence would be the only problem to consider. This is far from being so. In psychotherapy, presence is a mixed blessing. Patients often experience it, in their transferences, as controlling, invasive, voyeuristic, manipulative, punitive, or a critical form of surveillance that leaves them no place to hide. The regularity of appointments can be felt to be oppressive; consequently, the experience of breaks in the schedule may include relief, too. Partly or mostly, the difficulties of presence stem from what the patient projects, although the therapist's countertransference can contribute to the difficulties, as when she or he assumes a rigidly omniscient, anxiously comforting, or impassive posture.

Other problems arise in response to presence: for instance, the patients' fears of forming attachments that would leave them vulnerable to painful rejection or disappointment once they reveal "the ugly truths"; also, their fears of dependency, rage, and complete loss of the object; further, many feelings of being unworthy of their psychotherapists' care or concern or else feeling humiliated by it; and, to name only one more problem that I mentioned earlier, the patients' fears of their own benevolent feelings that would lead to giving up the paranoid and masochistic position from which they have been deriving security and perverse pleasure, even if at the cost of conscious psychic pain.

In response to these problematic aspects of presence, patients often tend to sexualize the therapeutic relationship or at least to intellectualize its sexual implications. It seems that they hope to distract attention from issues that arouse far more anxiety and guilt. For example, they bring up such ideas as this: that the therapy will prove that they are "really" gay or lesbian, or that they are being seduced or stimulated to be seductive or exhibitionistic. The therapist must proceed cautiously on this terrain, neither rejecting these concerns out of hand nor swallowing them whole, for however defensive this sexualization may be, it is likely to be heavily invested in by the patient. Consequently, the psychotherapist does well to attend to these sexual concerns at the same time as he or she looks for ways to use them as an avenue of approach to other, more primitive issues mentioned earlier. These are the issues that, in one way or another, focus on absence and all that it implies about basic problems of human relatedness. Sexual intimacy of whatever sort is only part of the story and quite possibly not its major part.

CONCLUSION

I have tried to show how the psychotherapist is continuously present in the patient's unconscious fantasies, regardless of literal absence or psychical absence during sessions, but that *simultaneously* the psychotherapist might be represented as present though absent or absent though present. Unconscious modes of function tolerate these contradictions. Therapeutic interpretations that take these factors into account and that do not ignore the role of mutual projective identifications in the interplay of transference and countertransference are the interpretations that enable the psychotherapist to deal most effectively with the actual and imagined comings and goings that are unavoidable aspects of the therapeutic process.

CHAPTER 6

DEFENSES AGAINST GOODNESS

The air of analytic sessions is always thick with implications of goodness. On the one hand, many versions of "badness" pervade analysands' self-descriptions, actings out, and condemnations of others; these versions imply goodness as their alternative. On the other hand are hidden moral references to goodness in such common locutions as "good-hearted," "good intentions," and "it is good for me." Also, upon analysis, one encounters many usages that seem more or less removed from goodness and yet are freighted with moral or moralistic imperatives: "a good time," "a good game," and "a good session." Goodness flourishes as an idea and a value in that other reality, the internal world of unconscious fantasy.

For many analysands, experiencing and expressing goodness are felt to be moves into a danger situation. Consequently, they erect defenses against these experiences. In this way, they may seriously limit analytic change. Certain analysands enact this problem in the transference through consistently self-injurious transgressions, uncomprehendingness, and negative therapeutic reactions. They also try to evoke negative countertransference in order to block their analysts' perception of their goodness as well as justifying their own denial of their analysts' goodness. Unconscious defenses against goodness therefore warrant the closest possible clinical study.

Although conflict over goodness is not unfamiliar to experienced analysts of all persuasions, goodness is not generally recognized as a technical psychoanalytic term. In Kleinian discourse, however, goodness *is* a technical term, with a set of referents that may be subsumed under *the depressive position* (Klein 1940, Steiner 1993). The depressive position features taking responsibility for others perceived as whole objects, concern and reparative intent, gratitude, generosity, reciprocity, and patience. In each analysis, these general referents serve as narrative headings that are individualized in storylines specific to each analysis (Schafer 1992).

Goodness enters into discussions of the feelings and fantasies that make up the analysand's internal world of object relations. In envy, for example, the envious subject is viewed as attacking the goodness of the object, spoiling it or even eliminating it by poisonous, biting, besmirching, or belittling fantasies and perhaps behavior as well. Goodness also figures prominently in discussions of the difficulty of emerging out of the omnipotent, persecutory, projective, and concretistic paranoid-schizoid position (Klein 1946) and entering the more mature, whole-object-related depressive position. In that advanced position forms of mature oedipal triangulation can develop.

Especially when they are moving toward and working through the depressive position, with all the concerns, responsibilities, and guilt feelings that go along with the joys of mature love, the analysands in question present massive reactions against feeling, believing in, and avowing openly personal goodness and the goodness of their primary objects who now are beginning to be grasped as separate, whole figures. Analysts find that their own goodness—their respect, care, dedication, empathy, and so on—is attacked by these defensive analysands either through denial, cynicism, and mistrust, or through defensive idealizations.

Nevertheless, analysts must assume that fundamentally these analysands are ambivalent in relation to goodness. That ambivalence is the spur to genuine analytic work, though its open emergence may be blocked by formidable defenses. The analyst who forgets this ambivalence may well be enacting negative countertransference, perhaps a retaliatory disowning of concern for the analysand's well being.

False goodness is another important aspect of struggles with goodness and will be discussed and illustrated later on. Also to be discussed later is the probably inevitable intrusion of conformist values into the analyst's dealing with goodness and the defenses against it.

CLINICAL EXAMPLES

Although the brief examples that follow vary in how much detail they include and in the complexity of analytic interpretation developed, they do illustrate different manifest forms of defenses against goodness. They also indicate the roots of those defenses in unconscious fantasy.

Ted

Ted, by now a familiar figure in this book, known to be an emotionally dry, obsessive person, is reflecting on his suppression of feelings, particularly compassion: "If you show compassion at all, it will become a lot. When emotion breaks out, it could release an avalanche. It's not a question just of expressing it, but even admitting it to myself. It goes with my need to feel tough." On another occasion, Ted is reflecting on the question of competence: "I am always surprised when I do something well. I'm surprised by my own competence. Why? I know I'm competent. It's nice to feel that if I put my mind to something and make an effort, I probably do it better than most other people. It's like when I took on that new assignment."

In this context, Ted may be viewed as doing more than linking goodness to compassion. He is also indicating that, in his psychic reality, there is goodness in taking initiative rather than just passively doing assigned jobs. By venturing out into the open on his own, he takes on the challenge of constructive, reciprocal, whole-object relationships. His curtailed spontaneity ties in with his rigid defense against feelings in general, pride and compassion among them. He must stop the avalanche that he fears will follow any freedom (presumably on an anal model of release of feeling).

Beth

Beth, a young woman, had become impatient and irritated with her mother over her mother's apparent insecurity. Her mother had been needlessly asking for guidance and permission to do things. Then, as though to generalize and diffuse the point and relieve her own subjective discomfort, Beth says that she has been feeling intolerant toward everyone. Returning to her mother, she adds, "She obliges me to respond by asking if what she is doing is okay." When I express interest in hearing more about this, Beth reports that, in this respect, she herself is like her intolerant father, and what's more, she and her mother even get pleasure out of their bickering.

I then remind her that our previous extended work on the transference has helped us see how she had picked up much of the sadomasochistic pattern of her interactions in her family. For example, in her effort to get close to her father and become his favorite, she had identified with him in a number of ways, including his sadomasochistic leanings. Beth begins to cry, rebuking herself for being "mean" to her mother in just the way her father is. She says, "My father doesn't let anyone get close to him; at best, he treats them like pets." Ruefully, she then adds, "Actually, of the two of them it's my mother that I can get close to." I then point out that she would be afraid of her father's reaction if she should show good feelings toward her mother in a direct way, so she can only use bickering to get close to her and have pleasure with her.

Conceivably, I would have been more analytically helpful had I verbalized her implicit transference reference, specifically, her experiencing *me* as distant; however, I decided not to do so because repetition in the transference had been a prominent part of the general context in which this session was taking place. For example, not long before, it had emerged that, after my return from a brief absence owing to illness, Beth had suppressed a spontaneous impulse to say that she hoped I was feeling better. She acknowledged having been worried about me, but she had had to maintain total silence on that topic. She explained that she had not wanted to be "presumptuous" by acting "familiar." She had assumed consciously that my rules forbade and condemned any relaxed spontaneity that would amount to presumptuous familiarity. I inferred that she had used projective identification to maintain distance from me. Beth was trying to make this awkward situation

95

my problem, not hers. Later, she came to understand this defense by reversal, and she used it less often.

Further analysis of Beth's projective identification led to her acknowledging her wish to be spitefully withholding of any informality of manner, in this way courting my dissatisfaction with her and blocking any sense of her goodness. Beth's defensive stance required that she forestall any behavior that might suggest that she was being sexually seductive toward me. She imagined that any seductiveness at all would stimulate traumatic interactions between us of the sort to which she had once tended to expose herself. In this respect, she was exercising the kind of caution about feminine appeal that was featured in her relationship with her father.

Thus emerged a link between the struggle against goodness and the dilemmas of the oedipal triangle. As noted, goodness is a constituent of the attained depressive position. That position requires a reasonably high degree of separateness from one's objects and a capacity for intimacy with them that paves the way into the clear triangulations of the mature oedipal situation and into the fears of its sexual and hostile consequences. Beth's trials and tribulations with her mother, as exemplified above, show an important aspect of the painful ambivalence of the oedipal girl toward her mother and how it is used to avoid getting "too familiar" with her father.

Dave

Dave, an obsessive analysand, continuously doubted his marital feelings: maybe he could have found someone better, an ideal woman. Self-reproachfully, he argued that this doubting showed him to be not much of a husband.

However, at this point in Dave's analysis, he was able rather readily to return to his pleasure in his wife, and he said, "She's good for me." Then, he realized with a start that saying that not only implied that he was expressing a need for her, but, more important, it implied his having any needs at all.

From the standpoint of defense against goodness, I would emphasize that his attack on his own good feelings toward his wife implied an attack on his good feelings toward me, this attack consisting of his endlessly doubting the results of much previous analytic work. Our work had shown other sides of his defensiveness, especially guilt over emancipating himself from his parents' control and his experience of me as another controlling figure. Soon, as we shall see, Dave brought in the additional problem created by the love object's goodness.

He began another session complaining that he felt more depressed, and then he mentioned that, on the way to his session, he had briefly imagined a smile of his mother's that seemed to him very sweet and girlish; he liked it. As we went on, I had occasion to mention that this image seemed to express his having deflected a feeling of that sort from both his wife and me. Seizing the opportunity I had given him to avoid the connection to me (was I uncomfortable with the image of me as girlishly sweet?), Dave responded to the point about his wife. He reported that she used to complain about his being too involved with work, spending too much time at it. When he then stood up for himself by pointing out her exaggerations, she backed down, saying that he means too much to her to continue to make a big issue of his work routine.

In the midst of telling me this, Dave became openly tearful. Tearfulness was not at all a usual thing. He said he has been touched by the signs that she gives him that she needs him; *he had never felt needed before.* He thought particularly of his father's lack of expressiveness and his own fear of being disappointed, and also of his mother's somewhat distracted and unpredictable though superficially conscientious caregiving. Gradually, we related this material to his problem of recognizing his own needs. He fights these needs because he anticipates being disappointed (see Chapter 2). At this point, Dave indicated a dim recognition that one disappointment itself does not necessarily undermine the continuity of a caring or loving relationship. As we worked this point over, I emphasized that one of his needs was to be needed. As the session progressed, his spirits improved visibly. Later on in the analysis, there surfaced as an important element in the transference: his need to be needed *by me.*

At this time, however, the goodness of the object was only just beginning to appear openly, as were Dave's own good feelings in showing signs of pleasure and deep responsiveness; earlier, there had been only intellectualized doubt-ridden remoteness. More of his defensiveness soon showed itself.

I arrived fifteen minutes late for the next session; he was my first appointment and I had been unavoidably detained. I found him already in the waiting room. He explained that he had found the door to the office suite open and had just walked in. I noted to myself that this was an unusual liberty for Dave to take; however, I said nothing, waiting to see how he would handle my lateness and his having taken this initiative. At first, he said nothing directly about either of these matters; instead he started talking about his difficulties with his wife. She has been feeling very burdened at work at this time, and to express his concern, he had volunteered to spend the whole weekend at home with her instead of spending time in his office working, as was his custom. He then reported to me that, at the very moment he had made his offer to her, he had begun thinking regretfully about what he would be missing at work. He began discussing this switch in his attitude self-reproachfully: it was more evidence of how altogether unfeeling he was in his marital relationship. Once again he felt that he was not much of a husband.

Soon he felt blocked, and only then did he mention my being late, wondering if he had something on his mind about it. What ensued was his presenting me with things he had wondered about while he was waiting, such as whether there was something wrong with me or if he had made some mistake about the time. Soon he confessed that he had been hesitating mentioning that for a brief second he had felt worried about me. In a dismissive tone, he quickly added that it was probably related to his fear of being dependent on anyone.

I expressed interest in his having found it hard to tell me about that worry. In response Dave developed the idea that it would signify more involvement with me as a person and would even show that he was enjoying our relationship, but, he added, that would be "personalizing" it instead of limiting it strictly to our working toward the goals of the treatment. Any such feelings made him uneasy. I asserted that he would experience his personal concern for my welfare as involving us in a very direct contact. He promptly tried to slip away from this theme by talking dismissively about the narcissistic nature of both his need to be dependent and his defense against it; for example, he pointed out, it had taken him half the appointment before he had even mentioned my lateness.

At this point I missed an opportunity to point out Dave's slipping away from the theme of closeness; instead I brought him back to this theme directly and reassuringly, saying that he *had* allowed himself on his own to get around to mentioning his worry and open up the subject and that, to me, his having done so suggested that, with all his ambivalence about it, he was not *altogether* walled off in this regard. I now believe that my shifting away from his explicit focus on defensiveness in the transference explains why, a moment later, he manifestly shifted away from himself and me and talked of his mother. He said that he has reworked his sense of his mother, seeing her now as someone who would think of him in terms of looking after him in order to do the right thing but then quickly turning her attention away to things that mattered more to her.

This point was not new, but this time he was deeply moved as he made it. With considerable emotion, he expressed an acute feeling of deprivation in relation to her. I noted to myself that Dave had never been this openly emotional and needful during the preceding years of analysis. At that moment, he was wiping his eyes frequently. Then, trying to get some distance from his feelings, he emphasized that a child learns how to be from the way the parents are. In what I now regard as an unnecessarily and disruptively comforting way, one that expressed my overidentification with him at that moment, I then said that it must have been intolerable to live constantly with the feelings of deprivation and anger at the very people on whom he had to depend; his parents were his only resource at that time so he must have had to adopt some kind of strict defense to make life bearable. Only then did I return to the transference—more than a bit too late—adding that that defensiveness is just what we had been working on in *our* relationship.

In these sessions, along with evidence of Dave's relaxing his massive defenses against feeling sad, needful, and angry, and against seeing the object's goodness, there was evidence of his beginning to relax his equally massive defenses against his own goodness. He also showed something of what he feared this relaxation of defense would lead to: a set of intolerably painful feelings.

I discovered the following week that he had repressed the emotional climax of this series of sessions. At first, he did not even remember that we had had these discussions. I believe this forgetting was based on several factors: his fearfulness, his preferred defense of forgetting, his being in a transitional phase, which would lead him to be in constant flux, and, I believe, his defense against my invasive countertransference.

Upon reflection I concluded that, on top of all that, Dave's repression must have been reinforced by my not having taken up the relation of this material to another of his feelings about my being late: I, like his mother, had been shallowly and unreliably attentive to him; I had left him alone to wait, worry, doubt himself, and do too much on his own. Both his anger at me and his fear of showing it had left him feeling hard pressed. I had lost my poise in the session and had become too engrossed in trying—counterproductively—to reassure and comfort him and, I think, myself. My almost entirely forgetting the transference at certain points was equivalent to a second forgetting of him. Dave's reaction to my analytic abandonment of him implicitly verified my ill-timed, "feelingful" reconstruction: he forgot the whole thing. This type of erasure is often evident when the analyst's countertransference interferes with analysis of defense.

FALSE GOODNESS

The characteristics of what I call false goodness emanate from the paranoid-schizoid position. Defensively, the

101

analysand tries to simulate the functioning of someone stably situated in the depressive position. At every turn, then, the analyst is confronted by pseudomaturity. As termination approaches, analysands often present false goodness to ward off painful feelings of loss, inadequacy, disappointment, and fears for the future. Persisting omnipotent fantasies and envy might also be concealed in this way. Chapters 7 and 8 develop this point further. Additionally, this simulation may well signify an attempt at a forced feeding of the "depleted" analyst as well as a fantasized redefining his or her gender by this pose of reversing roles of strength, power, and supplies. What is not in evidence then is the cluster of affects surrounding mature interest in, and convincingly distressing concern for, the object. Consequently, the undeceived analyst begins to feel up against a ruthless do-gooder who will get reproachful, uneasy, and self-critical if his or her offering is not received gratefully.

For example, a male analysand was hyperalert to every conceivable sign of my discomfort or distress, such as an occasional light cough, sneeze, yawn, or sigh, a bit of motor restlessness, and traces of disorder in the consulting room. He was afraid that his omnipotent, hostile controllingness had been overstressing, depleting, and ultimately destroying me. Consciously, he worried that he should not be presenting his self-concerns when all was not well with me. It seemed to me that was not so much guilt that moved him as fear that his aggression would lead to retaliation and abandonment. Coming out of the paranoid-schizoid position or perhaps a pathological organization (see, e.g., Steiner 1993) this false goodness involved much projective identification of needfulness, weakness, feelings of receiving insufficient care, and anger. The projective identification was being used to maintain the fantasy of omnipotence: it must be the other, not oneself, who needs help and is wrought up; the self must have the magical, unfailing resources to remedy all illness, injury, and incapacity. The fears of retaliation also involved projection of resentment and envy of my well-being and durability. For this analysand, his objects had to be carefully controlled so that he could proceed with this complex maneuver with the least possible distress.

Because a sense of falseness is a serious burden for many analysands, the analyst's close attention to it can be analytically productive and therapeutically beneficial. However, it is often difficult to distinguish clearly between true and false goodness, and, in many instances, the analysand's fluctuations yield mixed evidence. Another source of difficulty here is that goodness contains some elements of narcissism and projective identification (as in empathy).

Also to be taken into account is defensiveness in the countertransference; for example, not rarely, the analyst may have too intense a need to be a relatively selfless inhabitant of the caregiver role, and in that role she or he may too readily misread or mistrust an analysand's signs of budding goodness (as in a gift or coming early for a session). As usual, the question of degree—Freud's frequently mentioned quantitative factor—will confront each clinical judgment as to why, when, and how to intervene interpretively, if at all. And yet it must also be said that often the distinction can be made relatively easily owing to the prevalence, grossness and relative unyieldingness of narcissistic problems in the psychoanalytic transference. The following clinical example shows some genuine goodness, though falseness predominated at the moment.

ESTHER

Esther is a young professional with children. Shortly before a holiday she begins a session with the announcement that she will skip the last appointment of the week. As though changing the subject, she then says she is feeling guilty about my health. I look somewhat mussed up to her, and she thinks I am not well. She criticizes herself for putting me in the position of a servant, someone used by all my patients thoughtlessly. She likens it to her being like a baby who uses her mother whenever she needs her. Esther goes on to criticize herself for other forms of thoughtlessness and self-indulgence. Missing the point, I remark that she seems to be feeling bad about leaving me alone, neglecting me by extending the holiday absence. Initially she seems to agree, but she then says that perhaps I could die in the interval. She is appalled by this thought because she recognizes that she would be thinking primarily of its being a loss to her. By going on in this way she seems to be defensively propitiatory, but she also seems to be rightly questioning my assumption that it is specifically guilt she is feeling.

She continues to criticize herself for not paying enough attention to me: "You must get sick of that, all your patients using you." She begins to think how they use me by projecting all kinds of things into me; however, she makes a slip of the tongue, saying "production" when she intended "projection." Esther's associations to the word production go to *creation*, then *giving birth* to a child or a work of art such as a picture, but especially *bearing a child*. "It's something that emanates from your body. If I produce you, you come from me and I am responsible for your existence or your lack of it if I'm not attentive enough." As though retreating from the omnipotent idea of murder by neglect, she begins to feel sleepy and fatigued, and she wishes I would cover her. Finally, she gets around to saying how sick and tired she is of taking care of people. When I comment on her having trouble accepting her own wish to be taken care of, Esther agrees, saying that this wish is altogether "ignoble." In my own thoughts, I understand her to be suggesting that omnipotent strivings and shaky self-esteem are more consequential now than feelings of responsibility; nobility is her grandiose narcissistic aspiration.

I now regard this interaction as having shown that, *in this context*, Esther was manifesting mainly false goodness. To a large extent—I would not say entirely—her show of concern for my well-being was expressing her omnipotent fantasies (creating me) and a defense against her feeling both needful and murderous. The needful feelings were embodied in the not quite warded-off fantasy of her as a baby, my baby.

It is warranted to conclude that this was not an instance of adequately developed goodness; rather, it seems to have been mainly Esther's using shows of goodness to defend against parts of herself that she could not accept and integrate. Simultaneously, she feared that I, too, could not integrate them. She was trying, unsuccessfully, to deploy the defense of caring for others to cover her own needfulness. It is noteworthy that, despite Esther's recognition that she characteristically imposed burdens on herself, she switched rapidly from caregiver to complaining of being burdened by others. And in my inconsistency, I colluded with, and perhaps further stimulated, her defensiveness. Nevertheless, it seems correct to say of Esther that the relatively stabilized goodness of the depressive position did not seem to be freely available to her at that moment.

105

DISCUSSION

Because the idea of goodness is vulnerable to being expressed in the countertransference as a carrier of demands for submission and social conformity, it is important to reflect on usage. First, it is not useful to take an essentialist and universalistic view of goodness, such that it would make sense to ask, "What *is* goodness?" In clinical work, one does best to focus attention on each analysand's implicit and explicit usage. That usage always mixes conventionality and individuality. In theory construction, the analyst designates certain general attributes of fantasy, feeling, and behavior as referents of such general terms as goodness. These attributes serve as narrative headlines that must be developed through individualized storylines.

Second, it is analytically useful to study the genealogy of the analysand's usage. Doing so deepens the analyst's understanding of present psychic difficulties by allowing him or her to construct a fuller moral, ethical, object-related account of the analysand's history and present status.

The individualized course that I recommend is the traditional one. It limits the analyst to remaining an investigator of language usage and the narrative constructions it both allows and blocks. Individualization entails the recognition that analysands, analysts, and analyses differ to such an extent that what is convincing in one instance may not be so in the next. Thus, it is not always generous to be generous; the act may be felt to be presumptuous, extravagant, or burdensome. It is not always good to show compassion; that act may be felt to be humiliating or based on the projected fantasy of suffering. Help offered to an envious person who is in need of help may be experienced as instigating further envy. The "kindness" shown by a person clearly lodged in the paranoid-schizoid position is more likely to be an act based on denial of envy, a show of omnipotence, and fear of retaliation for past acts of aggression. Many contemporary critical theorists in the humanities and social sciences follow the same strategy of studying current usage and its genealogy while avoiding essentialist approaches to the big words.

Third, so long as he or she stays in role, the analyst should not aim to solve or avoid the eternal philosophical problems of ethics. One cannot hope to arrive at an absolute, value-free position. Analysts must accept and try to be cognizant of the permeation of language by values; one cannot transcend them. Still, it cannot be denied that analysts and analysands often belong to the same social class, intellectual class, and gender, and so are members of the same subculture or the same general culture; that being so, both may too readily take for granted many things that pertain to goodness. For example, both might tacitly agree that it is an act of goodness always to be kind, generous, patient, concerned, or sensible in particular cir cumstances, and as a result they might limit their analytic inquiry only to disruptions of those kinds of "goodness." The rest would be considered self-evident.

Ernest Jones (1955) reported that Freud subscribed to the position, "What is moral is self-evident," and we must assume that, mistakenly, Freud must have taken a narrow segment of society as representative of the whole; for he did not raise such questions as "Moral for whom?" "Moral under which conditions?" "Moral in which case?" and "Who is making the decisions and under which constraints?" It is, however, also possible to overestimate this danger of taking too much for granted. This essay has been a call for vigilance, not disruptive hypervigilance.

Finally, goodness does not present a unique problem. Many big words—trust, mistrust, despair, reassurance, improvement, and too many others to list here—present the same mix of conformity and individuality, thereby offering opportunities for the analysand, the analyst, or both, to turn an analytic dialogue into a veiled form of sermonizing.

CONCLUSION

Clinical work can benefit greatly from the careful analysis of defenses against goodness. Not rarely, analysands avoid the experience and expression of positive reactions to the goodness of others, and they hide good feelings of their own that could be expected to elicit the goodness of others. Envious wishes to spoil good objects, attachments to bad objects, defenses against gratitude and dependence, so-called negative therapeutic reactions, and other such conflictual factors help avoid depressive anxiety by blocking out goodness. These analysands dread abandoning their narcissistic, omnipotent, sadomasochistic, persecutory, paranoid-schizoid positions and moving toward mature depressive positions. That shift of position, notwithstanding the gratifications it makes possible, is viewed as imposing intolerable burdens on the internal world: loss, guilt, responsibility, felt ambivalence, and vulnerability to humiliation and disappointment.

CHAPTER 7

EXPERIENCING TERMINATION: AUTHENTIC AND FALSE DEPRESSIVE POSITIONS

It has long been recognized that the process of terminating is stressful for analyst and analysand. Under ordinary circumstances, it is, of course, the analysand who feels far more pained in response to the sharp sense of loss occasioned by the impending separation. The analysand feels increased temptation to regress back into disturbed emotional positions that have been worked on extensively and even appear to have been worked through adequately. In these regressive shifts, primitive defenses will be intensified. She or he hopes that these changes will forestall such painful subjective correlates of separation as grief, guilt, feelings of disappointment and resentment, and fears for the future. Separation is conceived in all-or-nothing terms, physical separation being equated with total loss.

Psychically, however, things are quite different (see Chapter 5). Both consciously and unconsciously, the analytic relationship lives on for an extended period of time, if not permanently. In the internal world, whether as an internal object, identification, or both, the analyst remains a presence in the analysand's life. If not in the foreground, then behind the scenes, as it were, the analyst will be present as a helpful or critical resource. Under favorable conditions, the regression during and perhaps immediately after ending will be temporary, not extreme, and responsive to interpretation.

Even the prospect of termination can set this difficult and complex process in motion. That prospect can be an influential factor from early on in the analysis. For example, some analysands defend against feeling involved in the relationship because, defensively, they keep in mind that it will end and that it is paid for; they hope that that way of thinking about it will prevent its ever becoming "real" for them. Others respond defensively to early developments in the transference that stimulate anticipations of danger; they dread the prospect that their analytic gains will bring them to the brink of deeply painful and ominous areas of anxiety, guilt, shame, dependence, perhaps even violence and madness, and they turn their thoughts prematurely toward termination. In other instances, the analysand's recognition of partial gains might stimulate a sense of triumph that is then expressed in manic gestures toward termination—"finished in record time!"

In an effort to supplement so much established knowledge in this most important part of analytic work, I have centered this essay on one *defensive* organization that is commonly encountered during periods when, on whatever basis, termination is in the air. I call this defensive organization *the false depressive position*, by which I refer to a pseudomature manner of coping with the stresses and strains of termination, one that serves as a wall that obstructs the analysis and also diverts it from essential issues even as the analysand gives every appearance of wanting to go on with the work.

To throw into sharp relief the main features of this defensive posture, I will first take up the chief characteristics

110

of the position it simulates: the depressive position. Also, because the specifics of termination must be understood as codetermined by both participants, and because at these times the analyst's countertransference might also veer toward the false depressive position and, on that account, stimulate or at least support the analysand's recourse to the same defensive posture, I will scrutinize the analyst's functioning, too.

To conclude the development of my theme, I will present two clinical examples of analytic work that took place when termination was being anticipated. One analysand demonstrates greater resiliency than the other, but both manifest the pseudomature concern, responsibility, reparative orientation, and other such features that characterize this defensive organization. Also, in both cases, though to different degrees, the analyst's countertransference appears to play a noteworthy role.

Also to be kept in mind is the fact that even when termination is not an active issue, painful loss can be experienced during all those separations that take place during analysis: between appointments; over weekends and holidays; and times when the analyst, the analysand, or both are psychically absent while physically present (see Chapter 5). Consequently, analyzing the bad feelings occasioned by separations of every kind prepares the analyst to understand and deal with the wide range of phenomena inevitably encountered during the process of termination.

Before beginning, I cannot emphasize too strongly that analysts usually deal with more or less intermediate, fluctuating, and mixed versions of the authentic and false depressive positions. Upon analysis, individual versions of these positions prove to be complex and not altogether internally consistent or coherent; nor is each identical with others that warrant the same general designation. However, if the analyst employs sharply defined, perhaps extreme reference points in instances of this sort, she or he will be better able to follow the analysand's associations. These reference points enable the analyst to remain oriented to what is momentarily predominant, though also unstable or fleeting. I will present the two positions—authentic and false—in their ideal forms.

THE DEPRESSIVE POSITION

The depressive position (Klein 1940, Steiner 1993) comprises numerous aspects of psychical function, the entirety of which would fit a conventional idea of maturity and an ego-psychological idea of ego strength. Fluctuations from the depressive position veer in the direction of the paranoid-schizoid position (Klein 1946, Steiner 1993). The paranoid-schizoid position corresponds to the cognitive and emotional functioning assumed to be characteristic of a young child, especially when that child is under stress or in conflict: immature defenses and synthesizing ability, weak self-boundaries, a proclivity for magical thinking, emotional lability, exaggerated projections, and so on. This position also corresponds to Freud's (1915a) account of the unconscious and to many accounts of the psychoses, including Freud's in the same 1915 discussion. Here, we will not be concerned with the developmental and diagnostic applications of the paranoid-schizoid concept because they are out of place in the present functionally oriented context. Also, in light of the contemporary research and understanding, both comparisons are open to numerous challenges.

A general overview of the depressive position must single out the following overlapping features (overlapping because they refer to different levels of function and possess different degrees of generality): reduced reliance on splitting and projective identification; reduced emphasis on those narcissistic needs for omnipotence that imply intolerance of dependency needs or of any recognition of limitations or imperfections of the self; reduced inclinations to become envious; the achievement of whole-object experience as indicated by a prevalence of loving over sadomasochistic desires and fantasies; a relatively stable tolerance of the ambivalence that inevitably accompanies relationships; heightened concern for others and the self as shown in readiness to assume responsibility, feel appropriate guilt, and implement reparative aims; relatively sustained ability to think symbolically and perceive realistically; dependable capacity to mourn and tolerate separateness, differences, and the independence of objects from one's own control; and differentiated and relatively stable recognition of the parental couple as forming a union from which one is excluded, which is to say, signs of having moved beyond oedipal crises, though not necessarily beyond the influence of oedipal prototypes on later object relations.

My frequent use in this summary of such words as relatively and prevalence indicates that it is not correct to attribute to anyone full, totally stable occupancy of the depressive position: none of us occupies the depressive position completely and permanently; each of us remains vulnerable to flux, as we see especially clearly in connection with the termination of even the most beneficial analysis.

Another feature of the depressive position that is usually implied rather than stated is the capacity to live in conventional time. This capacity stands in contrast to the timelessness of unconscious mental processes. Living in conventional time means genuinely experiencing a past, a present, and a future instead of being limited mainly to the timeless state found during analysis among those who function mostly within the paranoid-schizoid position. In the usually timeless state of the paranoid-schizoid position, things, relationships, feelings just *are*. For example, defeat is *what* there is and *all* there is when it is defeat that is being experienced, excitement is *what* there is and *all* there is when it is excitement that is being experienced, and so on. Even such words and phrases as "always," "forever," "never," and "living in the past" do not adequately convey this timelessness, though they are often used for this purpose in clinical discussions. They are the kinds of terms that would be used by an outside observer in a rational position, one who does not fully enter imaginatively into the analysand's timeless state.

Thus it is that in the transference, for example, the "all good" analyst can quickly become the absolutely and always "all bad" analyst once there has been a lapse of empathy or a time away from the analysand. The analytic past seems to vanish completely; there is only *now*—more exactly, *is*. The conception of a "good but also bad" analyst (Jacobson 1964) is to be found only within the precincts of the relatively more mature depressive position, as is the ability to expect a departing analyst to return. Winnicott pointed out somewhere that for these timeless analysands, the analyst who comes even a little late stimulates the feeling that he or she will never come.

Therefore, the alert clinician will not take for granted the analysand's explicit references to the past, present, and future, for in primitive mental states or on the primitive levels of function that underlie surface integration, these references are best regarded as vestigial or essentially intellectualized. They have little emotional resonance, and they play no significant role in mental functioning and action in the world. It was to this recognition of living in time as an achievement of analysis that Loewald seemed to refer when he said, "In the daylight of analysis the ghosts of the unconscious are laid and led to rest as ancestors (1960; see 1980, p. 249).

Ideally the analyst begins to contemplate the possibility of termination when signs appear that the analysand has moved well along toward the depressive position, however conflictually this move has been made. One sign that the analysand might be ready is her or his referring to, or hinting at, thoughts of termination in the absence of desperation, resentment, or manic excitement. Ordinarily, depressive anxiety blocks movement in this direction, for it arises as soon as the burdens of maturity are recognized and anticipated. Only after it has subsided sufficiently can there develop genuine responsibility, concern, guilt, and deeply felt mourning. It might be the analysand who first mentions termination or it might be the analyst. In either case, the analyst must exercise restraint when dealing with this prospect. Tact, timing, and dosage, as recommended by Loewenstein (1982), are never more important. To function in this manner, the analyst, too, must have developed pretty much past the point of acute depressive anxiety and attained relative stability in the depressive position.

Most analytic discussions and presentations do not spell out what it is for the analyst to be in this desirable position. Its constituent elements have been specified only when countertransference has led to a disruptive enactment. Then, the observer—it may be the self-observing analyst—accents the negative of the depressive position. Mention might be made of lapsed tolerance of ambivalence, ambiguity, and indeterminacy; disappearance of curious, caring, and responsible attitudes; inability to maintain neutrality or equidistance from the constituents of intersystemic and intrasystemic conflict (following Anna Freud's [1936] mode of formulation); decrease of patience; violation of ethical requirements; irrationality; impaired personal integration; and reliance on the primitive defenses and omnipotent fantasies that lead to manipulation and persecution of the analysand. Converting those negatives into their positive counterparts, we arrive at a pretty accurate account of what it is that shows the analyst to be maintaining or approximating the depressive position in general and when dealing with termination issues.

Several more attributes of the analyst's authentic depressive position should be specified because, especially in these pluralistic times, when classical theory has been critiqued and revised so extensively that its traditional identifying features have been obscured, if not discarded, we cannot take it for granted that specific analysts continue to consider these attributes essential or at least desirable. The first attribute is a firm belief that psychoanalyzing means trying to understand human development and functioning, especially in the analytic situation, as greatly influenced by *unconscious* desires, fantasies, and conflicts. The second of these additional attributes is a firm belief in the importance of the method of *free association* in providing the cues that indicate these presupposed unconscious influences.

A third essential attribute is a firm belief in the central, if not exclusive, role of interpretation and emotionally experienced *insight* in promoting deep-seated change in the direction of *adaptation*, adaptation being understood to range far beyond adjusting to prevailing circumstances and taking in changing these circumstances or seeking others that better serve one's interests (Hartmann 1939). A fourth and equally valuable factor is the analyst's conviction that, unconsciously, the analysand will defend against change vigorously, persistently, and often with great subtlety, this self-protective stance manifesting the analysand's heavy investment in avoiding new and old danger situations and preserving sadomasochistic attachments to "bad objects."

On the basis of these beliefs, the analyst is prepared to seek, detect, and interpret coherence and continuity in what seems to be either a changing sequence of topics or mere clinging to a fixed topic. He or she is also prepared to treat intruding thoughts and feelings not as interruptions but as addenda to what is being taken up; they are addenda in the sense that often they can be viewed as further elaborations expressed in other terms. The analyst with no pressing fear of going mad can work with associations in this way, steadily adhering to Freud's hypotheses concerning unconscious mental functioning. Believing that it is almost impossible to change the latent topic, the analyst is not compelled to maintain what conventionally would be called "continuity" or "staying on the topic." The latent topic may, however, appear only in reverse, displaced, or otherwise disguised forms, some of which are temporarily or permanently unrecognizable; much may have to be left inadequately understood or totally misunderstood.

It is all a question of how one listens. The analyst who is relatively stably in the depressive position feels at home listening in terms of displacements, enactments, symbols, metaphors, and analogues in the "second reality" (Schafer 1985) of the internal world. Further, he or she does not doubt that it may take a while before the associations' implications and connections can be discerned, to the extent that they can be. Then, as in the case of a dream presented early in the analysis, they can be retold later in a way that fits them insightfully into a coherent narrative of the analysand's general problems and present subjective experience. Consequently, the analyst who is more or less in the depressive position can be expected to exercise appropriate restraint of overt action. She or he steadily manifests patience and a capacity for containment. At times, out of concern for tact, timing, and dosage, the analyst must defer (contain) even the shrewdest of empathic insights. For example, there are times when, as Betty Joseph (1983) has pointed out, the analysand seems unable to tolerate understanding and being understood.

My clinical examples will illustrate how these essential features get expressed in the analyst's readiness to accept in an integrated, positive way the realization that "that's the way it is," to accept yet another regressive shift, yet another turning against him or her, and yet another account of the analysand's entering into an untenable and painful relationship. Further, "that's the way it is" can express recognition and acceptance of the never-ending flux of psychic states between, on the one hand, the integrated and adaptive and, on the other, the primitive and maladaptive. And perhaps most of all, the analyst who works reliably around the borders of the depressive position is ready to accept incompleteness, for at the time when termination is pending, the analyst must come to terms with the realization that the analysis has not intensively addressed, understood, and modified every significant issue; not every major problem has withered away; and all these issues and problems may continue to burden the analysand in the postanalytic period, though most likely to a lesser degree. Upon considering this incompleteness, the analyst who has not adequately moved toward the depressive position may feel guilty, futile, resentful, and aggressively critical of the self, the method of analysis, or the analysand (see Chapter 8). In contrast, the more securely based analyst recognizes that analysis is not an all-powerful tool for change and that it is not subject to demands for conformity to the analyst's favored social norms or to norms that are rationalized as prescribed by theory or by the analysand's relatives or significant others.

THE FALSE DEPRESSIVE POSITION

Analysands who simulate being in the depressive position tend to make conspicuous shows of concern for others and to dwell on their own sense of responsibility and their reparative intentions. At times, they so overdo these demonstrations that their recipients soon experience them as intrusive and burdensome or else as intent on holding them at a distance. Consequently, far from feeling held or helped, the recipients feel targeted, burdened, or isolated. One might say that instead of fitting in, these inauthentic analysands take over, and instead of being respectful and empathic, they are condescendingly and inattentively sympathetic. The self-centered expressiveness of it all casts a pall over the social situation, making it clear that, unconsciously, the would-be helpers are seeking security by enclosing themselves within narcissistic fantasies of omnipotence. That is why they react with anxiety, depression, an apologetic stance, mistrust, aloofness, belligerence, or some combination of these when they do not get the hoped-for, confirmatory gratitude—more exactly, submission.

In the treatment situation, these inauthentic analysands are likely to be hyperalert to every sign of the analyst's discomfort: a sneeze, a yawn, a shift in position, some bit of disorder in the consulting room or in the analyst's physical appearance or dress. These ambiguous cues are turned into occasions to express concern or regret for overtaxing and depleting the analyst; the analysands might then apologize for forcing the unwell analyst to work on their problems when they should be granting the analyst some reprieve from the stress of analyzing. (A clinical instance of this sort was cited in the preceding chapter.) The implicitly pressured quality of this show of compassion gives away its being based on an unconsciously maintained view of the analyst as weak, needful, vulnerable, contemptible, and consequently in need of care from on high. This posture derives in large part from projective identification of the analysands' own needfulness and feeling of inferiority, envy, humiliation, or deadness. It bolsters their fantasies of omnipotence, gratifies their envy, and perhaps soothes their fears of reprisal as well.

For example, one analysand who had assumed the false depressive position emphasized (with the help of some interventions by the analyst) that he, a young man, was so conscious of my age and so sure on that basis that I was fragile and needed protecting that he had to suppress and displace considerable resentment in the transference. This "kindness" served as a defense by reversal, and it also enacted his own unconscious belief that he could easily topple me and in fact was very likely to do so. It was he, not I, who occupied the enviable position. As might be expected, the prototype of this transference of bravado seemed to have been developed in relation to issues and figures in the analysand's early life.

Manifestations of the false depressive position are not always as obvious, sustained, or grandiose as the preceding description suggests. They can take subtler forms, and they might emerge only on occasion. For example, they might show simply as a too ready and too consistent agreement with, and productive use of, the analyst's interventions; then, it is as though the analysand is making the point that all conflict has been satisfactorily resolved, ambivalence is no longer a problem, and, accordingly, the analyst's interventions just do not stimulate pain, puzzlement, or opposition. To the analyst it seems that there is too much poise and not enough friction, reluctance, or uncertainty.

Earlier, when I discussed the depressive position, I suggested that it is just at this point that any instability or inauthenticity in the analyst's emotional position is likely to introduce special difficulties or intensify those already present. For example, the analyst who is impatient for excellent results will be inclined to be either perfectionistically demanding or idealizing of new and partial gains. And like the analysand, she or he may be obvious about it or extremely subtle.

Countertransferences are likely to be intensified in response to the stresses experienced by the analyst, too, during the termination process. She or he might be struggling with some feelings of grief, disappointment, dissatisfaction, and, now that the end is near, long suppressed resentment or envy of the analysand. Consequently, an analyst in the false depressive position is ill prepared to help each analysand experience termination as fully as that analysand can. For example, the analyst might not attempt to work through competently or completely the analysand's dissatisfactions, grudges, and envious feelings and jealousy of other and future analysands. In their unconscious fantasies, those others will be the more treasured babies or lovers or both. Instead of remaining analytical, the analyst might become persecutory or, in a manic way, omnipotently deny his or her own disturbed feelings. In other instances, the off-balance analyst who, in his or her countertransference needs some comfort or reassurance, might push a guilty analysand further into the false depressive position to the point where the analysand feels compelled to provide what the analyst requires: reassurance, practical help, and so on. It is not rare that the initial task of a second analysis is interpreting the termination of a first analysis in which the analyst's countertransference stood in the way of adequate working through.

CLINICAL EXAMPLES

Jane

Jane seemed to be approaching the subject of termination. In recent months, she had been functioning fairly consistently more or less in the depressive position. Although she still readily tilted toward a false position, she was able to regroup forces somewhat spontaneously and reestablish her own kind of integrated adaptiveness. This kind and degree of flux is not unusual during this pretermination phase of mixed excitement, poise, grief, and dread.

Jane had been lodged in the paranoid-schizoid position during much of her analysis. Her usual attitude toward others and herself had had a judgmental, all-or-none quality. She had clung to the idea that the fundamental rule specified a certain way of functioning on the couch as "good" or as constituting "working analytically"; for her to do otherwise was unforgivably "bad." Ironically, this conception of working analytically—trying always to control what she said—allowed her to avoid anything that felt to her like free association. She regarded free associating as giving up control, being manipulated into an unguarded position, and "surrendering" totally to her analyst. Also, this surrender would be the only possible result of her accepting interpretations of her projecting into the analyst her own harshly authoritarian internal objects and identifications.

Slowly, and after some years, change had become manifest. Jane was moving unstably into a less frightened, less defensive, and less masochistic position. At times, she expressed that shift toward maturity and adaptive use of her strengths by remarking, "That's interesting." In many instances, of course, "That's interesting" can be used to express a detached, intellectual, passive attitude; in her case, however, as demonstrated by her subsequent productions and emotional experience, it conveyed her commitment to develop further understanding. By "interesting" she meant, "This requires careful analysis." To the extent that she could sustain her new attitude, and often she did so impressively, she showed confidence that I would be thinking about her "interesting" material in the same analytic way, that is, searching for further understanding that would be helpful to her. In this shift, she was showing less reliance on projective identification of authoritarian demand and cruelty, moderation of that demand and cruelty, decreased omnipotence, and more identification with the analyst's nonjudgmental analytic attitude and his way of focusing on what seemed to be analytically significant moments.

On this basis, she could begin bringing fresh and deeper material without having omnipotently figured out in advance what she thought were sufficient explanations of what she was reporting. Now she was often able to continue talking without being driven to "see" or seek "important" connections as a way to close out further possibilities, including her possibly needing the analyst's timely interpretations. She was less the victimized, neglected, suffering analysand, and she was better able to allow herself to experience guilt consciously. For example, she felt guilt in connection with a newly emerging sense of her primal love and concern for, and identification with, her mother. This freedom did not entail greater emotional distance from her much-beloved father; rather, it rendered more complex her long-entrenched, simplistic idea of her emotional position as a child.

It was only then that she could recognize with appropriate pain and resentment that she had always felt that her own dependent needs had never been met. For instance, as a little girl, she had "accepted" that, instead of needing and expecting her mother's help, she was to blend helpfully into her mother's emotionally exhausting preoccupation with her own business affairs. But she could play this role only ambivalently, and as a result, she had regularly aggressed against her mother in deed and fantasy, much of it in the form of positive oedipal rivalry. With this sense of her history, she was indeed an aggressor and had much to feel guilty about.

At the time to be discussed, Jane was having trouble sustaining these changes toward the depressive position. For example, on one occasion it slowly became evident that she had begun viewing the progressive changes just described as pushing her toward a much-feared termination. In response, she began to revert to a familiar and "safe" paranoid-schizoid position. She manifested great fear of the unknown after termination. Although she did not mention termination explicitly, she did indicate between the lines of her conscious material that it was in her thoughts and so it would be wise to adopt the policy, "the less said about termination the better!"

The specific context of this regressive shift was this. Recently, and on the basis of better integrated and more realistic functioning, she had learned that in order to conclude some business dealings that she had initiated independently, she would have to ask a hated, persecutory, hith-erto-avoided partner to sell at a reasonable price his inter-est in some jointly owned property. To her surprise, when she brought herself to ask, the partner raised no objection to this sale. Jane experienced this seemingly fortunate development as a "shattering piece of news." She then ex-plained that, although she had indeed attained what she wanted, now she would not only have to collaborate with her partner on the deal, she would have to acknowledge that he could be "good." With dismay, she announced that abandoning her negative image of him would affect her very badly, because for a very long time she had needed to confine him in her scheme of things to the role of a purely hateful person.

In response to her dismay, the analyst then said that just as in all her close relationships, especially her relationship with him (the analyst), it was sometimes hard for her to tol-erate mixtures of good and bad. He then reminded her of her evident ambivalence about taking the lead in proposing this desirable deal. He also mentioned a topic that had come up for analysis frequently—her gross use of splitting "good" and "bad" and projecting the "bad" when considering both him and her parents, and he emphasized that now, once again, she was faced with the (to her) grim necessity of tol-erating complexity and ambivalence. Significantly, even when she was in the midst of this regressive shift, Jane did not lose her readiness to adopt the attitude, "That's inter-esting." She was open about her dismay and her need to maintain a persecutory stance, and she was ready to re-flect on the intensity of her negative attitude toward her partner's favorable response. Earlier in the analysis, she could not have responded that way.

When Jane was closer to termination, she added to her reflective comments, "That's the way it is." Then, no longer high-pitched, she could develop relatively straightforward descriptions of problematic situations. Authoritarian judgments and painful resignation no longer dominated so many of her narratives. "That's the way it is" could be understood as an expression of her readiness to accept ambivalence and loss of omnipotence while retaining initiative, hopefulness, and trust. For example, after she had thrown a birthday party for a friend single-handedly and then had had to be up all night to handle an emergency in her business, she came to her session saying, "I'm just too tired to do analysis." She noted at once that she was not feeling anxious or guilty about taking this position, and she added reflectively, "That's the way it is."

Leading up to the moment of Jane's asserting and accepting her being exhausted was her focusing intermittently on how all her life she had been trying to ward off guilt; now she could usually see clearly that her habitual way of warding off guilt had been to hide it behind "shame and blame." She understood that she had evolved these hiding places in the service of her automatic use of fantasies of omnipotence and her two-way persecutory attitudes. She had relied heavily on splitting and externalization. By projecting her own self-disapproval, she had been able to feel unified in the consciously familiar role of the self-righteous victim of others. Had she remained in that position in this session, she could have acted the part of a drudge trying to go on "working" despite her exhaustion, blaming her analyst for his demandingness, and feeling ashamed of her "failing" at analysis, and all the while she would have kept on secretly feeling superior. Recognizing her gains in integration, reflectiveness, and trust, the analyst felt at ease letting her do it her way.

It was also noteworthy during this phase of the analysis that Jane could allow herself to be deeply touched by her

aging and ailing mother's need to be close to her. She did
so even while her mother continued to disappoint her
painfully, just as she had always done. Her mother lost
things, she broke things, and she was painfully unresponsive to news of Jane's business successes. Previously,
Jane would have focused on the destructive hatred implied
in her mother's being that way, and she would have felt all
the more justified in her having, as she saw it, trium-
phantly stolen her father's affection from her mother earlier in life and inwardly treated her mother dismissively.
Now, even though Jane could feel hurt and resentful in
response to her mother's actions, she could recognize that
"That's the way it is," meaning "That's the way *she* is," and
she could then go on to see herself differently. For example, she could remember that in her early years she had
not turned exclusively toward her father; she acknowledged that she had gone back and forth between her parents, feeling love, alternating with despair and anger, for
both of them in response to their narcissistic and destructive ways.

In the session I reported, it was noteworthy that, despite
her tiredness and lack of motivation, she did go on to "do
analysis," but she did so spontaneously and ungrudgingly.
She gave no sign that she was being self-sacrificially and
submissively "good," nor was she self-conscious about
having "done analysis." Nevertheless, that she was worried
about all this change could be inferred from her not having
gone on explicitly and spontaneously to link her expressed
ambivalence and guilt to the transference. Believing that
she had already taken on quite enough autonomy for one
session, and also because time was up, her analyst let it go
at that.

The next day, however, it became evident that he had
misjudged the state of her transference—and his coun-

tertransference. Jane began by saying that the room was too chilly; she felt cold and asked if it would be okay to turn on the radiator. He took this opening to mean that she was feeling distant and uncared for. In order to bring out her feelings, he questioned why she had to ask about that now in view of the fact that in the past, it had been clearly established that if she felt cold, it would be okay just to turn on the radiator; she did not have to ask for his okay. In her regressive way, she ignored his comment and replied that she had not wanted to be rude, and then, to drive her defensive point home, she added that she had not wanted to make him physically uncomfortable by overheating the room. Drawing on some work they had done in the past, he responded, "You can't think that I always treat you like a guest whose comfort always comes first." She said, "Being treated that way is such a rare experience," and went on to explain with much feeling that while she could accept the idea of being a guest, that by doing so imposed a requirement that, unfailingly, she be on her best behavior.

The analyst realized then that Jane was letting him know that she had retained a good-sized chunk of the old expectation of harsh treatment; consequently, it was important that he remember that she was not wholeheartedly in favor of her new gains. These gains were still threatening to her. He also inferred that she was letting him know that it would have been useful in the previous session to develop the link to the transference, for she was now showing him in action what both of them had deferred the day before, namely, noting explicitly that he was not to take for granted the stability of her shift toward the depressive position. Certainly, he should not get excited about termination, with all it implied about leaving her on her own, as he had done the day before.

The analyst responded by reflecting inwardly on whether or not he was manifesting some countertransference impatience for stability of position, if not for termination itself, and then decided that, in his radiator interventions, he had indicated some impatience by not interpreting her feeling neglected. Notwithstanding this provocative countertransference, the atmosphere in the second session had remained mostly collaborative. She did not persist in maintaining the artificial maturity of the false depressive position she had manifested by her bringing up the radiator in the "polite" and "caring" way that she had.

Esther

My second clinical example, Esther, it will be recalled, was discussed in the preceding chapter as showing false goodness. Authentic goodness being an attribute of functioning in the mode of the depressive position, its false version qualifies as one form of rigid and unconvincing pseudomaturity in the context of termination. When Esther was in a late phase of her analysis, she was usually able to maintain her hard-earned depressive position when under stress. At times, however, she would regress rapidly, though transiently, to the paranoid-schizoid position, meaning that she could then slowly and independently work her way back to her more mature position. In her regressions, Esther particularly favored the false depressive position that had been, and to some extent had remained, an ingrained part of her character. During this late phase of the work, her regressions seemed to be precipitated more readily as, after long putting it off, she began to let herself experience and recognize classical positive oedipal desires and fantasies in the transference.

She behaved as though this new consciousness threatened her entire sense of herself; it threw into question every one of her self-justifying accounts. That was much too much.

In the larger context of the analytic process, Esther may be understood as feeling threatened by two interwoven developments. The first was the pending termination, which she experienced consciously as a total separation that could only bring to an end her transferential mixture of residual omnipotence and victimization. The second was the emergence of the oedipal triangulations. That change could only have intensified her correlative feelings of defeat, loss, and guilt. Previously she had been able to ward off these feelings by omnipotent reparativeness and feelings of superiority and control in the analysis and in her enacted oedipal triangles. Only at this point, and only in an unstable way, was she able to acknowledge these painful factors. It may have been precisely this approach of the separation represented by termination that revived and intensified her unconscious oedipal experiences and facilitated their clear appearance so late in the analysis. Almost certainly, the timing had led her to think of the holiday weekend that lay ahead as a preview of the termination that would end her fantasized dyadic grip on her analyst. Separation would undermine the omnipotent control that included oedipal victory.

In the context of termination, Esther's analytic gains had become shaky, but they had not collapsed irreparably. As in the case of Jane, the analyst had apparently conveyed some countertransference pressure toward termination, this time by being too ready to perceive as guilt a veiled narcissistic display (see Chapter 6). His being out-of-tune could have further stimulated her regressiveness.

CONCLUSION

Optimally, consideration of termination begins after the analysand has been functioning fairly reliably more or less within the depressive position and shows resiliency when regressions occur. But no sooner is termination mentioned or even anticipated then the analysand's reactive anxiety stimulates another defensive regression. That shift may be responsive to countertransference cues. One such defensive shift is assuming a false depressive position, that is, simulating a mature, caring, balanced, "well-analyzed" mode of relating to others, often doing so in a burdensome, aggressive, and disappointing manner. The defensive aim is to escape the complex, often painful experience of separation, loss, and responsibility occasioned by termination. At that stressful time, however, it can additionally involve an effort to fit in with the analyst's also having defensively adopted a false depressive position. Thus, the analyst's emotional stability or lack thereof plays a central role in the analysand's experience of termination.

Terminations are a subclass of separation experiences. When the interpretations put forward here are not recklessly generalized, they can advance the understanding of adaptive and maladaptive responses to a variety of separations. At the least, they can facilitate formulating the analytic questions it would be helpful to consider in troubled times, and it is no small gain when these interventions further the analysand's consolidation of beneficial analytic changes at the momentous time of termination and afterward.

CHAPTER 8

PAINFUL PROGRESS: THE NEGATIVE THERAPEUTIC REACTION RECONCEIVED

Making progress while undergoing psychoanalysis often induces painful anxiety and sadness. Analysands dread what lies ahead and mourn long-lasting commitments to themselves and others they are leaving behind. Now that they are changing their orientation to relationships and to themselves, they must work through shame, anxiety, feelings of loss, and guilt in the internal world. In reaction to these painful changes, they back away from opportunities for further progress and revert to manifestations of the maladaptive orientations they have been relinquishing. In the analytic lexicon, they are said to be engaging in negative therapeutic reactions.

The idea of negative therapeutic reaction has been a mainstay of psychoanalytic discourse since Freud (1923) introduced it. Earlier (1916) he had anticipated this conceptualization when he discussed, "those wrecked by success." In keeping with his emphasis on the centrality of the Oedipus complex, Freud regarded these wrecks and retreats as guilty acts of abandoning worldly and analytic gains that unconsciously signify forbidden oedipal gratification or steps toward oedipal victory.

Later, Joan Riviere (1936) published a well-known Kleinian treatment of this topic. Being less restricted to oedipal issues, her emphasis on guilt was much more inclusive than Freud's. I believe that most contemporary analysts continue to refer to negative therapeutic reactions—as I have done in earlier chapters—and they ascribe them now to a wide variety of painful feelings and apprehensive fantasies, guilt being only one of them. Among the others are fears of loss, rejection, or abandonment; envious and persecutory attitudes; and efforts to maintain absolute control over the grandiose tendencies stimulated by their worldly and analytic gains. They might then seek mediocrity, failure, and humiliation. Still, oedipal guilt, along with its regularly accompanying castration anxiety or one of its female equivalents, always remains an important factor to consider.

I believe, however, that the idea of negative therapeutic reaction, valuable though it is, has its theoretical and technical drawbacks. A critical review is overdue. In the three sections of this chapter that follow, I will undertake that review, concentrating most of all on the idea that it is not usually analytically useful to think of these reactions in negative terms. To establish a general context for my critique, I will first raise questions about Freud's theoretical and technical concept of *resistance*, for I believe, and have already argued in several places (1976, 1983, 1997a) that the idea of resistance indicates the presence of a negative attitude that compromised Freud's otherwise remarkably open-minded approach to his analysands. Second will be an expanded conception of the phenomenon that I consider systematically and neutrally analytic and therefore technically more useful. The third and final section will be devoted to four brief clinical illustrations chosen to illustrate my thesis, other dynamic issues being set aside for the purpose.

RESISTANCE

Using the term *resistance* implies that the analyst and the analysand are being viewed as adversaries. More exactly, *resistance* implies that, unconsciously, if not consciously, the analysand is refusing to do what the analyst wants and expects. The analyst who thinks in this way is abandoning the analytic attitude, no longer maintaining an unshakable and neutral curiosity about the beliefs, feelings, and intentions that unconsciously shape the analysand's controls and conduct, most of all in the analytic relationship itself.

I take this position while knowing full well that basically, *resistance* is understood to refer to *internal* conflict, the analysand resisting becoming aware of unconscious factors of importance: memories, desires, defenses, and so on. Ordinary analytic usage of the term does, however, highlight the manifestations of this conflict in the many forms of obstruction of the analytic process erected by the fearful analysand. It is in this respect that the relationship gains its adversarial coloring. With this understanding, I continue my critique.

The analytic attitude underlies the analyst's steady and appropriate search for *reasons*. In this respect, the analyst's orientation remains affirmative, not negative—affirmative not in its denying negative thoughts and feelings, but rather in its seeking to define that which the analysand is trying to accomplish through seeming or being unproductive or disruptive. If, then, the analysand blocks, evades, attacks, fails to remember, or does something else that seems negatively inspired, uncollaborative, and implicitly defensive, analysts are most effective when they approach these problematic actions as signs of unconscious conflict that involve significant feelings of anxiety, guilt, shame, mistrust, dismay, or resentment.

Sometimes, these "negative" actions have been provoked in part by the analyst. Countertransference is always a relevant consideration in this context. Even so, after taking this factor into account, the analyst continues to search for reasons embedded in unconscious fantasy and conflict. For analytic purposes, the analysand's recalcitrance is to be regarded as manifesting a problem that has not yet been understood. When there is open opposition to the work and enticement to engage in a power struggle, the analyst wants to know what the analysand is trying to accomplish thereby, not stopping at what the analysand is trying to avoid. In keeping with the analytic attitude, the analyst takes the appearance of opposition to be merely the surface of the analysand's troubled situation, that is, manifest content to be understood in terms of its latent meanings.

Freud understood enough about this problem to consistently emphasize the importance of analyzing the resistance, not fighting it head-on (1912a,b, 1914b, 1915b). Unfortunately, however, in his formal discussions he exemplified the analysis of resistance in a quite limited way; it amounted to telling the analysand that he or she is in a state of opposition about something and that this opposition is the reason for the current disruption, and further, that the analysand is probably doing so as way of withholding some unexpressed thought and feeling about the analyst (Freud 1912a,b). More than being limited, this kind of intervention implicitly tries to bypass defense analysis and simply force transference into the open. Over the years, analysts have learned to go beyond this way of approaching resistance. Now, if they maintain their emotional balance, they tend to view manifest opposition as the next significant development in the analytic process. The situation does not call for instruction or "breaking through"; instead, it awaits understanding and interpretation.

Going further in these earlier reviews of resistance (see especially 1997a), I then argued that Freud's abundant use of martial metaphors in discussing the analytic relationship evidenced a personal need to conceive it in adversarial terms. Freud seemed to have clung to this adversarial stance notwithstanding (1) his many demonstrations of profound empathic understanding of the trials and tribulations of existence along with its thrills and joys, (2) his strong endorsement of the idea that the analyst should value empathic understanding as a way to reach analytic goals, and (3) his later emphasis (1926) on the danger situations of childhood and their manifestations in the current transference. In these respects, Freud showed his genius; still, he valued *resistance*.

Consequently, Freud can be viewed as splitting his ambivalence, that is, failing to integrate his thoughts and feelings about the work of analysis. I attribute some of this splitting to his zeal in demonstrating the therapeutic potential of his method. That zeal appears to have made him an impatient analyst. I attribute some of the splitting to another factor: Freud's needing "good" results, such as recovery of memories and relief from symptoms, to amass data for his theory of psychopathology, developmental and existential problems, and the normal forms of socialization that grow out of the primarily instinctual psychic states of infants that he had postulated.

On the basis of these views, I then recommended that, because *resistance* implicitly supports an unhelpful stance in the countertransference, it be put aside and replaced by the concept of *defense*. *Defense*, which is specifically geared to the analysis of conflict, does the essential work that Freud claimed he did with the concept of resistance, and does it better. I added that, if a third term must be added to the foundational terms of the psychoanalytic process—defense and transference now being the first two—countertransference should be the third. Thus: defense, transference, and countertransference triangulate the analysand's functioning in the clinical situation.

NEGATIVE THERAPEUTIC REACTION OR NECESSARY DEFERRAL?

Because negative therapeutic reaction is a technical term, it requires us first of all to be clear about the kinds of clinical situations for which it is designed. I realize that these situations are observed and described differently within different psychoanalytic perspectives; however, in pursuing my argument I will remain within the borders of the traditional Freudian-Kleinian method, the method that champions interpretation by an empathic but neutral and more or less emotionally reserved analyst. That is the method I favor and therefore know best.

As in the case of analyzing defense, it is essential that the analyst take it as a principle of doing analysis that, in the analytic situation, a sense of great danger permeates the analysand's unconscious fantasies. Underlying states of conflict develop and repeatedly give rise to painful feelings. If not encountered directly, these feelings are clearly implied in the extreme measures that analysands take to ward them off. One might say that the feelings are very present in their conspicuous absence. Sometimes they are first encountered in the analyst's countertransference, in which case they may be taken as signs that the analysand has successfully split and projected problematic feelings into the analyst and perhaps enticed the analyst into an enactment.

On this view, the analytic process is almost always colored by a dread of understanding and of personal change. Because progress is painful, the analysand is to be understood as clinging to a maladaptive psychic equilibrium based on symptoms, disordered character features, sadomasochistic attachment to that which induces conscious suffering in self and others, as well as covertly protecting personal assets and productive use of available opportunities for establishing a place in the world. The analysand is also viewed as trying to convey or project not only the worst aspects of destructiveness, both self- and other-directed, but also the most intense feelings of love, desire, and dependence that have been turned into overwhelming threats by other conflicts and by previous painful life experience.

Why, then, should the analysand feel at all free to join the analyst in entering and exposing that menacing world of unconscious fantasy, desire, and conflict? Indeed, it can be said that analysands cannot give truly informed consent upon beginning analytic treatment, for at that time they can have no conscious awareness of what "dangers" lie ahead: treatment probing deeper and deeper into themes of dependence, fragility, hatred, loss, abandonment, forbidden desire, grandiosity, envy, and ruthlessness, as well as frightening feelings of excitement and love and "perverse" or otherwise socially unacceptable desires. If, during the process, analysands draw back from fresh suffering, if they reverse direction and undo the presumed gains of the clinical work, what warrant has the analyst to consider them as behaving negatively? To be sure, the analysand's doing so is a reaction against the changes that are taking place, but it can be *negative* only in the eyes of the overzealous analyst. This is the analyst impatient for what she or he considers to be good results, progress, or success.

139

In this subtle way, Freud's word for it—*negative*—lends support to whichever narcissistic strivings for omnipotence inhabit the analyst, and it also might be used to justify unwarranted frustration over the seeming thwarting of his or her best analytic efforts. Analysts who lean in this unanalytic direction view "negative therapeutic reaction" as a good way to describe an analysand's cutting off fresh material and undermining beneficial changes that are already under way. They see it as a refusal or regrettable retreat, and at times they feel it as a smack in the face.

Earlier I mentioned Joan Riviere's (1936) Kleinian paper on negative therapeutic reactions and said that, over the years, it has proved unnecessary to stick to guilt or oedipal-level dynamics to explain them. Much of this development may be attributed to the foundational work of Melanie Klein (1975) and its elaboration by her creative followers (see the collections in Joseph 1989, Spillius 1994, and Steiner 1993; see also Feldman 1990, 1994). In their vocabulary, *negative* is in comparative disuse. Mainly they focus on intense preoedipal or pregenital feelings, including guilt, though they do not view the stages of development in question as *pre*oedipal or *pre*genital in that they interpret oedipal and genital issues and guilt in the years of life preceding the mature Oedipus complex and its "resolution." Early guilt usually centers on fantasized hostile attacks on the mother's body parts, her relationship with father, and all those siblings—real, imagined, and anticipated—who have issued from her womb or could.

Other limiting factors include envy and ingratitude and the unconscious fantasies in which they are expressed, such as having already damaged the mother and her significant others. In the instance of envy, the helpful analyst, having been linked unconsciously to the split-off, idealized good mother or her breast, becomes the target of wishes to spoil that helpfulness (see Chapters 4 and 6). One way to accomplish this spoiling is to damage the treatment by regressing from signs of progress. Additionally, part of Riviere's discussion emphasizes tenacious attachment to "bad objects." Thus, the Kleinians have enriched not only the approach to analyzing regressive reactions to the pains of progress, but also Freud's more general account of danger situations.

CLINICAL ILLUSTRATIONS

Ted

Ted, with whom we have become acquainted in several earlier chapters, would regularly forget what we had talked about from session to session. Indeed, he would forget even more and with extra persistence after any session that included the least suggestion of intense feeling or sense of relationship with me. For a long time, Ted remained uncomprehending when I pointed to the accumulation of indications that his functioning was disrupted in response to my absences over weekends and during holidays and vacations. Even when he would accept a tentative, limited interpretation, he was compelled to modify it to the point where it would lose the imprint of its having come from me. Narcissistically, he would somehow change my insight into one he had achieved on his own.

I understood this maneuver to be one of his many ways of precluding any experience of dependency or gratitude. Ted's capacity to maintain emotional stability and capable functioning in the external world seemed to depend on his acting only in accord with an unconscious fantasy of a completely self-sufficient life carried on in a cocoon-like

141

environment. On this basis, his work record was, in fact, one of significant achievement.

Additionally, Ted manifested signs of a persisting intense attachment to his parents. Implied in his notion of this attachment was a fantasy that, though dead, *they* depended on *him* and *they* were vulnerable to *his* comings and goings. Thus, he experienced considerable guilt whenever he began to enter into other relationships, and this guilt did seem to play a part in his regressive reactions to analytic advances.

Consequently, I could infer that, by acting toward me as he did, Ted was showing me his dilemma. I began to understand that, in an oblique way, he was collaborating with me in his treatment by making his dilemma available for interpretation. That collaboration was also evident in his exceptionally regular attendance over a long period of analysis and in the great seriousness of his realization that he had reached a point in his life where he stood very much in need of someone else's help to get out of what he experienced as a dismal rut. Showing me his omnipotence-in-a-cocoon could be considered his saying to me, "Don't you see what I am up against?!" Ted was engaged in a project far more complicated than simply reacting with guilt to any sign of progress or success.

Jim

Jim, our next example, grew up in a family consisting of a hypercritical mother and a weak, boastful, and unreliable father. It seemed that he had grown up without adequate parental support for ordinary self-esteem and self-confidence and that at an early age he had taken on the burden of keeping his parents pacified, each in his or her own way. Like Ted, Jim had developed a very strong stand against experiencing his own needfulness. That defense seemed to be protection against disappointment and rage. As such, it seemed to be his only method of maintaining his precarious integration.

Jim's solution led him, unconsciously, to assume the role of an omnipotent figure in his social and work relationships. He always had to be the helper, the smarter one, and the soothing one. In his analysis, however, Jim spoke of himself with enormous self-consciousness and self-criticism. He watched his every move and reconsidered his every utterance suspiciously. Even his self-derogations were suspect. This mistrust seemed to manifest intense attachment to, and some identification with, a bad object—his hypercritical mother—much as Riviere described. Also, a good deal of Jim's apparent self-mistrust was devoted to curbing any sign of identification with a father who commanded no respect in the family and no trust in the son.

With this pathological organization of experience, fantasies, defensive positions and also achievements, desires, and values, Jim had to find subtle ways to conduct himself as a "superguy" in the analysis, too. He did so even though, in the content of his remarks, he kept complaining about his behaving that way. Also, in addition to treating himself suspiciously, by projective identification he cast me in a hypercritical, dictatorial role. In this defensive and accusatory transference, he would not accept interpretive comments for what they were. He could not accept the recommendation that he try to speak in a free-associative manner instead of feeling committed always to having a set of topics "to discuss." In other ways, too, Jim did his best to ward off a situation in which he could in any way become exposed to me, or trustful, dependent, respectful, worthy of respect, spontaneous, or grateful.

143

Nevertheless, over time, Jim began to gain some relief from the extreme and chronic physical and mental tensions that had led him into analysis. Even then, however, he could not acknowledge that these benefits might have anything to do with the analysis. Indeed, each time he might have acknowledged the benefits of analysis, he would soon find a way of immersing himself in a situation that would increase his physical and psychical pain.

Jim was not without memories of having had some good experiences growing up in his family, but he could barely recognize that the support he derived from analysis—from me—could be a factor in his present functioning. Instead, he kept busy documenting his bleak family story with old and new material and remained seemingly impervious to my efforts to initiate a mutually recognized analytic process that could be therapeutically beneficial.

As with Ted, I believe it would be inappropriate to view Jim's analytic conduct as negative in any sense. Whatever guilt there was in his conduct was, I thought, just one element in a complex psychic situation. His unconscious fantasy of omnipotence precluded gratitude.

I must add that these analysands and some others I will mention briefly are usually presented under the heading of severe narcissistic disturbance. But this set of problems and tendencies is so commonly encountered that my continuing emphasis here should not be regarded as a highly selective account of only one kind of analysand. The problems and tendencies are also prevalent, though perhaps less glaring, in analysands who present themselves as neurotic characters, symptomatic neurotics, reactive depressives, or mildly addictive personalities. Thus, to one extent or another, the examples of Ted and Jim are applicable to a wide array of analysands. It is a question of how one looks at each of them, and what one is inclined to designate the area of basic disturbance. For so many analysands, Freud's oedipal-centered model of negative therapeutic reaction just does not seem sufficiently inclusive.

Kitty

As a third example, I mention a young woman, Kitty, the daughter of an infantile mother who seemed to me to have identified with her to a pathological extent. Kitty's account suggested that her mother was trying to live through Kitty as a way of opening up for herself a new set of opportunities for personal growth. As analysis of Kitty's repressions, denials, and anxieties progressed, it came to seem that way to Kitty, too. A reversal of generations describes much of the dynamics of this mother–daughter relationship (Jones 1913). To the extent that Kitty's mother tried to assume or carry out motherly functions, she was inconsistent, competitive, destructively envious, and burdensome.

Necessarily, this family configuration entailed considerable thwarting of Kitty's dependency needs. As happens so often during a childhood spent in this kind of setting, Kitty developed a deep and ambivalent attachment to this apparently totally unsatisfying figure and, in later life, sought to create similar relationships with others—in the analysis, with me.

Consequently, my interpretive efforts on Kitty's behalf could only be met with great apprehension, resentment, tempestuousness, and also some relief. Most of the time, manifest negativity and guilt over moves toward emancipation were outstanding features of the analytic sessions. Fundamentally, she seemed to be expressing ambivalent identification with her mother based on disappointed love.

145

Kitty was carrying on the family tradition. Often, she reacted dramatically to imagined slights. From time to time she rapidly and apparently totally destroyed any previously established analytic rapport or mutual understanding. However, the disappearance of whatever had been gained in analysis was more apparent than real. She was showing volatility, not perishability. Still, her increments of improvement were very small, and her regressions dramatic. It took a considerable amount of time before she could sustain her analytic advances.

Fred

Fred, our final example, the son of a remote father and a cold, narcissistic mother, had been brought up to be a perfect gentleman in an austere New England manner. Fred played this role in his transference relationship. On this basis he did his best to lure me into enactments that would confirm his fantasies of the analytic relationship as nothing but a repetition of times past. It was important for him to be the implicitely resentful, defiant, and also despairing son in the transference, as though he had to be dealing with someone from whom he could only expect great remoteness or below-zero coldness. Like the others reported on in this chapter, Fred, too, struggled mightily against any sign of gain. He regarded progress as adjustment to intolerable parenting.

CONCLUSION

Were analysts to refer consistently to the clinical problems addressed in this chapter, they would speak of regressive reactions to the emotional pain that, along with relief, excitement, and pleasure, inevitably accompanies progressive analytic change. Briefly, they would speak of *painful progress*, the title of this chapter. Those who are analytically informed would understand that this designation implies the potential for regressive reactions. Painful progress would not imply oppositional or combative postures on the part of both participants of the sort suggested by Freud's terminology and martial metaphors. Consequently, these analysts would react empathically and with renewed curiousity to analysands' resorting to regression to make manifest their dread of where they sense they now are and what lies ahead if they continue to go on changing.

AFTERWORD

Psychoanalysis is not a form of psychosurgery. It does not extirpate bad feelings. Bad feelings come with being alive. Every one of us must deal with grief, envy, disappointment, the other painful experiences that have been discussed in the chapters of this book, and many more as well. That we can often defend successfully against experiencing these bad feelings consciously does not enable us to lead untroubled lives, for a price is paid for heavy reliance on this emotional tactic: impoverishment of liveliness in the internal world and in personal relations with others.

What psychoanalysis can do is reduce the painfulness of unavoidable bad feelings and increase tolerance for psychical pain. It can facilitate gaining freedom from frightening, vengeful, and guilt-ridden unconscious fantasies; improve reality testing; decrease reliance on passive, masochistic, regressive modes of functioning; and increase tolerance of pleasure in the body, relations with others, the use of one's assets, and pride in achievement. Attachments to bad objects and the feelings they generate decrease. These changes balance or outweigh those emotional pains we inevitably suffer by being in the world, and they help us feel that it is worth our while to live a lively existence, even if it is not always satisfactory or free from pain. By changing the world one constructs, by reshaping the remembered past, and by expanding the range of safe, gratifying, and possible futures, analysis makes it so that experience is no longer overloaded with bad feelings, now that the capacity to love is no longer stunted, desperately denied, or otherwise seriously compromised.

REFERENCES

Ablon, S. L. (1990). Developmental aspects of self-esteem. *Psychoanalytic Study of the Child* 45:337–365. New Haven, CT: Yale University Press.

Abraham, K. (1921). Contributions to the theory of the anal character. In *Selected Papers of Karl Abraham*, pp. 337–392. New York: Basic Books, 1953.

——— (1924). A short history of the development of the libido, viewed in the light of mental disorders. In *Selected Papers on Psychoanalysis*, pp. 418–501. New York: Basic Books, 1954.

Abrams, S. (1990). Orienting perspective on shame and self-esteem. *Psychoanalytic Study of the Child* 45:411–416. New Haven, CT: Yale University Press.

Bergler, E. (1948). *The Battle of the Conscience: A Psychoanalytic Study of the Inner Workings of the Conscience*. Washington, DC: Washington Institute of Medicine.

Britton, R. (1989). The missing link: Parental sexuality in the oedipus complex. In *The Oedipus Complex Today: Clinical Implications*, ed. R. Britton, M. M. Feldman, and E. O'Shaughnessy, pp. 83–191. London: Karnac, 1994.

——— (2001). The role of envy in stifling creativity. Unpublished.

Feldman, M. M. (1990). Common ground: The centrality of the Oedipus complex. *International Journal of Psycho-Analysis* 71:37–48.

——— (1994). The dynamics of reassurance. *International Journal of Psycho-Analysis* 74:275–285.

Frankiel, R. (2000). Envy and the dangers of difference: Panel report (summarized). *Journal of the American Psychoanalytic Association* 49:1391–1404.

—— (2001). On depression, shame, and the envious superego. Unpublished manuscript.

Freud, A. (1936). *The Ego and the Mechanisms of Defence.* New York: International Universities Press, 1946.

Freud, S. (1893–1895). *Studies on Hysteria. Standard Edition* 2:1–335.

—— (1900). *The Interpretation of Dreams. Standard Edition* 4/5:1–626.

—— (1905). *Three Essays on the Theory of Sexuality. Standard Edition* 7:125–244.

—— (1909). Notes upon a case of obsessional neurosis. *Standard Edition* 10:183–318.

—— (1910). The antithetical meaning of primal words. *Standard Edition* 11:153–162.

—— (1912a). The dynamics of transference. *Standard Edition* 12:97–108.

—— (1912b). Recommendations to physicians practising psychoanalysis. *Standard Edition* 12:109–120.

—— (1912c). *Totem and Taboo. Standard Edition* 13:1–161.

—— (1914a). On narcissism: An introduction. *Standard Edition* 14:67–102.

—— (1914b). Remembering, repeating, and working through. *Standard Edition* 12:145–156.

—— (1915a). The unconscious. *Standard Edition* 14:161–215.

—— (1915b). Observations on transference love. *Standard Edition* 12:157–171.

—— (1915c). Instincts and their vicissitudes. *Standard Edition* 14:109–140.

—— (1916). Some character types met with in psycho-analytic work. *Standard Edition* 14:309–333.

—— (1917). Mourning and melancholia. *Standard Edition* 14:237–258.

—— (1920). *Beyond the Pleasure Principle. Standard Edition* 18:1–64.

—— (1921). *Group Psychology and the Analysis of the Ego. Standard Edition* 18:65–143.

—— (1923). *The Ego and the Id. Standard Edition* 19:1–59.

—— (1925). Some psychical consequences of the anatomical difference between the sexes. *Standard Edition* 19:241–253.

—— (1926). *Inhibitions, Symptoms, and Anxiety. Standard Edition* 29:77–105.

—— (1927). Fetishism. *Standard Edition* 21:152–158.

—— (1933). *New Introductory Lectures on Psycho-Analysis. Standard Edition* 22:1–182.

—— (1937). Analysis terminable and interminable. *Standard Edition* 23:209–253.

—— (1940). *An Outline of Psycho-Analysis. Standard Edition* 23:139–207.

Gillman, R. D. (1990). The oedipal origin of shame. *Psychoanalytic Study of the Child* 45:357–375. New Haven, CT: Yale University Press.

Hartmann, H. (1939). *Ego Psychology and the Problem of Adaptation.* New York: International Universities Press, 1958.

Heimann, P. (1950). On countertransference. *International Journal of Psycho-Analysis* 31:81–84.

Horney, K. (1924). On the genesis of the castration-complex in women. *International Journal of Psycho-Analysis* 5:50–65.

Isaacs, S. (1948). The nature and function of phantasy. *International Journal of Psycho-Analysis* 29:73–97.

Jacobson, E. (1946). The effect of disappointment on ego and superego formation in normal and depressive development. *Psychoanalytic Review* 33:129–147.

—— (1964). *The Self and the Object World.* New York: International Universities Press.

—— (1971). *Depression: Comparative Studies of Normal, Neurotic, and Psychotic Conditions.* New York: International Universities Press.

Jones, E. (1913). The phantasy of the reversal of generations. In *Papers on Psychoanalysis* (5th ed., pp. 407–413). Boston: Beacon Press, 1961.

—— (1955). *The Life and Work of Sigmund Freud,* vol. 2. New York: Basic Books.

Joseph, B. (1983). On understanding and not understanding. *International Journal of Psycho-Analysis* 64:291–298.

—— (1989). *Psychic Equilibrium and Psychic Change: Selected Papers of Betty Joseph,* ed. E. B. Spillius and M. Feldman. London: Routledge.

153

REFERENCES

Klein, M. (1935). A contribution to the psychogenesis of manic-depressive states. In *The Writings of Melanie Klein*, vol. 1, pp. 262–289. London: Hogarth, 1975.

—— (1940). Mourning and its relation to manic-depressive states. In *The Writings of Melanie Klein*, vol. 3, pp. 344–369. London: Hogarth, 1975.

—— (1946). Notes on some schizoid mechanisms. In *The Writings of Melanie Klein*, vol. 3, pp. 1–24. London: Hogarth, 1975.

—— (1957). Envy and gratitude. In *The Writings of Melanie Klein*, vol. 3, pp. 176–235. London: Hogarth.

—— (1975). *The Collected Writings of Melanie Klein*, vols. 1–3. London: Hogarth.

Kohut, H. (1977). *The Restoration of the Self*. New York: International Universities Press.

Loewald, H. (1960). On the therapeutic action of psychoanalysis. *International Journal of Psycho-Analysis* 41:16–33.

—— (1980). *Papers on Psychoanalysis*. New Haven, CT: Yale University Press.

Loewenstein, R. M. (1982). *Practice and Precept in Psychoanalytic Technique: Selected papers of Rudolph M. Loewenstein*. New Haven, CT: Yale University Press.

O'Shaughnessy, E. (1999). Relating to the superego. *International Journal of Psycho-Analysis* 80:861–875.

Reich, A. (1951). On countertransference. *International Journal of Psycho-Analysis* 32:25–31.

Reik, T. (1941). *Masochism in Modern Man*. New York: Farrar, Straus & Giroux.

Riviere, J. (1936). A contribution to the analysis of the negative therapeutic reaction. *International Journal of Psycho-Analysis* 17:304–320.

Rizzuto, A. B. (1991). Shame in psychoanalysis: The function of unconscious fantasies. *International Journal of Psycho-Analysis* 72:297–302.

Rothstein, A. M. (1994). Shame and the superego: Clinical and theoretical considerations. *Psychoanalytic Study of the Child* 49:263–277. New Haven, CT: Yale University Press.

Schafer, R. (1968). *Aspects of Internalization*. New York: International Universities Press.

—— (1974). Problems in Freud's psychology of women. *Journal of the American Psychoanalytic Association* 22:454–485.

—— (1976). *A New Language for Psychoanalysis.* New Haven, CT: Yale University Press.

—— (1983). *The Analytic Attitude.* New York: Basic Books.

—— (1985). The interpretation of psychic reality, developmental influences, and unconscious communication. *Journal of the American Psychoanalytic Association* 33:537–554.

—— (1992). *Retelling a Life.* New York: Basic Books.

—— (1993). Five readings of Freud's "Observations on transference love." In *Tradition and Change in Psychoanalysis*, pp. 57–98. New York: International Universities Press, 1997.

—— (1994). On gendered discourse and discourse on gender. In *Tradition and Change in Psychoanalysis*, pp. 35–50. New York: International Universities Press, 1997.

—— (1997a). *Tradition and Change in Psychoanalysis.* New York: International Universities Press.

—— (1997b). *The Contemporary Kleinians of London.* New York: International Universities Press.

—— (1997c). Conversations with Elisabeth von R. In *Tradition and Change in Psychoanalysis*, pp. 79–92. New York: International Universities Press, 1997.

—— (2001). Gender jokes/ Sexual politics. *Studies in Gender and Sexuality* 2:277–298.

Spillius, E. B. (1993). Varieties of envious experience. *International Journal of Psycho-Analysis* 74:1199–1212.

——, ed. (1994). *Melanie Klein Today,* vols. 1 and 2. London: Routledge.

Steiner, J. (1993). *Psychic Retreats: Pathological Organizations in Psychotic, Neurotic, and Borderline Patients.* London: Routledge.

Yorke, C. and collaborators (1990). The development and functioning of the sense of shame. *Psychoanalytic Study of the Child* 45:377–409. New Haven, CT: Yale University Press.

INDEX

lack of emotion in, 7–8
values in, 106–108
Loewald, H., 77, 115
Loewenstein, R. M., 115
loss, 89
  defenses against, 102, 111
  from termination of therapy,
    86, 109

Masochism in Modern Man
  (Reik), 22
masochism/sadomasochism,
  7, 22, 95
  expressions of, 11, 28, 73
  pleasure from, 3–4, 10
memories, idealized, 26
mental processes, 84, 113–
  115
mortification. *See* humiliation
  and mortification
mother, 127, 140, 143
  identification with, 46–47
  identification with daughter,
    145
  insecurity of, 94–96
mother–child relationships,
  58–59
motivations, 106–107, 135–136
"Mourning and Melancholia"
  (Freud), 60

narcissism, 17, 59–60, 81,
  130, 141
narcissistic damage, 5
negative therapeutic reaction,
  63–64, 91–92, 133–134,
  138–141

object relations, 60–61
  analyst in, 75–76
  development of, 58–59, 94
  and disappointedness, 18, 23
  goodness in, 92–93

objects, 96
  attachment to bad, 21, 117,
    143
  bad, 16–17, 22, 28, 37, 42,
    143
  good, 16–17, 20–22, 97
  internal, 21, 37, 42
obsessions, 96–101
oedipal desires, 129
oedipal triangle, 96, 130
Oedipus complex, 13, 57–58,
  140
omnipotence, 3–4, 29, 81
  analyst's, 140
  as defense, 8, 17, 130
  and envy, 66, 74–75
  and false depressive
    position, 199–120
  and false goodness, 102–
    103, 105
  and humiliation, 44–45, 47–
    48
  playing role of, 143–144
  and self-sufficiency, 141–142
  working through, 30, 35–36,
    123, 126
ostracism, fantasies of, 38

paranoid-schizoid position,
  92, 122
  characteristics of, 101–102,
    112, 114
  and humiliation, 43, 45, 50–
    51
  moving out of, 30
  object relations in, 59–60
  regression to, 124, 129–130
parents, 10, 34, 47, 64, 74,
  98, 142, 146
  dependence on, 32, 100, 142
  and disappointment, 21, 27–
    28, 127
  fanatical attachment to, 5–6